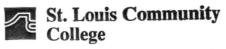

Beyond the
Dependency Culture

Recent Titles in
Praeger Studies on the 21st Century

Beyond the Dependency Culture

People, Power and Responsibility in the 21st Century

James Robertson

Praeger Studies on the 21st Century

PRAEGER

Westport, Connecticut

Published in the United States and Canada by Praeger Publishers,
88 Post Road West, Westport, CT 06881.
An imprint of Greenwood Publishing Group, Inc.

Printed in the United States of America

The paper used in this book complies with the
Permanent Paper Standard issued by the National
Information Standards Organization (Z39.48–1984).

10 9 8 7 6 5 4 3 2 1

English language edition, except the United States and Canada,
published by Adamantine Press Limited, Richmond Bridge House,
417–419 Richmond Road, Twickenham TWI 2EX, England.

First published in 1998

Library of Congress Cataloging-in-Publication Data

Robertson, James. 1928–
    Beyond the dependency culture : people, power and responsibility
in the 21st century / James Robertson.
        p.   cm.—(Praeger studies on the 21st century, ISSN
1070–1850)
    Includes bibliographical references and index.
    ISBN 0–275–96315–2 (alk. paper).—ISBN 0–275–96316–0 (pbk. :
alk. paper)

    1. Welfare state.   2. Public welfare.   3. Poverty.   4. Social
problems.   5. Social change.   I. Title.   II. Series.
HN65.R574   1998
303.4—dc21   97–53213

Library of Congress Catalog Card Number: 97–53213

ISBN: 0–275–96315–2 Cloth
       0–275–96316–0 Paperback

Contents

Foreword

by Ronald Higgins

Independent writer and lecturer on issues of global security. His books include *The Seventh Enemy: The Human Factor in the Global Crisis* (Hodder 1978 and 1982) and *Plotting Peace: The Owl's Reply to Hawks and Doves* (Brassey 1990).

A certain serious politician recently told me with shame that he rarely found time to read more than one substantial book a year. I shall tell him that this should be it.

There will be no apology for suggesting a collection of essays and lectures, nor even one stretching back twenty years. Many of the ideas in the earliest ones are as freshly apposite today as they were then. Some have already infiltrated the agendas of policy debate but need a fuller understanding. Others still await their time—just one mark of the author's originality.

Nor shall I allow my recommendation to be dismissed on the grounds that James Robertson and I are old friends (we have often disagreed, sometimes strongly) or that twenty five years ago we were both members of Whitehall's policy-making caste. (We were already both showing signs of sceptical non-conformity beneath our clerical grey suiting.)

Robertson's thought has the clarity and logical rigour of the best policy-makers but it rejects most of their easy assumptions, whether of left or right. He is a quiet revolutionary, throwing over the tables of inherited dogma. While he amply shares the general decline of confidence in governments and orthodox politics, he does not rest in the self-righteous passivity that afflicts so many. Instead, he re-addresses the age-old questions of what kind of society we want, nationally, regionally and globally, and how individuals can best help to achieve one where self reliance is a general reality, not a Thatcherite slogan with which to justify increasing inequality.

He sees a principal cause of dependency—and of the poverty, unemployment and environmental damage it causes—in the 'enclosure' by rich and powerful people and organisations of more than their fair share of resources and the consequent exclusion of the majority. He holds that citizens have not only individual rights but the right to an equal share in the commons created by society and nature at large. It is surely staggering that the denial of this proposition became commonplace in the last two decades.

Robertson's call for a post-industrial, post-modern revolution involves every aspect of life. The sheer range of these pieces is remarkable. Reading them will benefit questioners of conventional thinking in a multitude of fields including economic policy making, work, welfare, money, health, the environment and nuclear power. But none of his subjects are treated shallowly: faced with a self-assured dogmatism, Robertson has an eye for the jugular. More than that, he offers constructive proposals for change.

The book primarily concerns the nature, prospects and reform of the industrialised societies of Europe and North America—from which geo-political power is now shifting towards Asia. But the dominance of the prevailing Western ideology of hyper industrialism and unexamined 'growth' mean they no less concern Third World and hence global development too. Indeed in global terms, the maldevelopment of the Rich North is arguably even more profoundly serious than the under-development of the Poor South.

Over these twenty years, the author has been disappointed by the slow pace of change and perhaps become more conscious of the possibility of real catastrophe. Yet his passion and will for change remain clear. He sees our age as one of global, not just post-industrial, transformation involving a profound shift from dependency to co-operative self-reliance at every level, not least the local.

If this desirable and urgent transformation is actually to happen, we shall owe a great debt to daring yet systematic thinkers like him who have worked outside the great institutions and have seen the more vividly that the emperors have no clothes.

James Robertson has never accepted dependency himself and has become a powerful individual voice in the diagnosis and remedy of great but not inevitable evils. Not only politicians should read these lucidly written pieces: all thoughtful citizens—not least leaders of opinion—will do so to advantage.

Acknowledgments

Many people have helped me, in one way or another, to develop the lines of thinking in this book over the last twenty years. The names of some are mentioned in particular chapters and chapter prefaces. There are many others—too many to name—from whom I have learned. I have good memories of my associations with them. My gratitude is due to them all.

My warm thanks go to Jeremy Geelan who asked me to publish in this Adamantine series; to Sheila Moorcroft for her invaluable help and advice in shaping the contents and coverage of the book; and to Jason Pearce and Lloyd Allen who took charge of the layout design and typesetting.

I particularly want to thank Ronald Higgins, not just for his generous Foreword but also for our friendship and our companionship as independent thinkers since the 1970s. Escapees, in his case from the Foreign Service, in mine from the Civil Service, we have worked in complementary fields since his publication of *The Seventh Enemy* and mine of *The Sane Alternative* in 1978, he on the need for change in international security and foreign policy, I more on the social and economic sphere.

My special thanks, once again, are for my wife, Alison Pritchard. She and I have worked together throughout these twenty years. I am very grateful to her for everything.

J.H.R.
August 1997

Introduction

We need a new path of progress, based on co-operative self-reliance and not on the further growth of dependency. We need to create a world that empowers people (and nations) to take responsibility for their own further development in co-operation with one another. That is an important end in itself. It will also be the only means, barring worldwide catastrophe, of transforming today's ecologically destructive patterns of human activity into ways of life that can be sustained into the future.

That is the theme of the lectures and papers reprinted here. They span a twenty-year period from 1977 to 1996. They complement books published during that time—*The Sane Alternative* (1978, revised 1983), *Future Work* (1985) and *Future Wealth* (1990). They are selected from a large number of lectures and papers addressed to a variety of audiences and readerships. They reflect ideas about alternatives to dependency which have been gaining ground over that period, and are likely to be more widely accepted in the 21st century.

They are reprinted in chronological order, showing their dates. They are in their original form, except for one or two instances (indicated in the text) where passages have been left out to avoid duplication between one chapter and another. A few small clarifications and corrections have also been made, and a number of out-of-date references have been left out.

This Introduction, the Epilogue and a preface to each chapter were written in 1997. New footnotes to the chapters are distinguished from original footnotes by being dated 1997. Otherwise, I trust it will be clear that the text of the chapters reflects my understanding of the situation prevailing when they were originally written, not now.

The focus of this selection is on the industrialised countries of Britain, Europe and North America. The top priority for us who live in these countries is change in our own societies—not just to create a better future for ourselves, but to enable us to contribute to the future of the world as a whole. Thus, articles specifically concerned with global and Third World development have not been included. Neither have any papers written for The Other Economic Summit and the New Economics Foundation since 1984. A separate selection of these may be published later.

A shift from dependency to co-operative self-reliance will be an essential feature of a successful transition to a post-industrial, post-modern age. Chapters 1, 2 and 8 are about the processes of this historic transition and about the emerging new worldview that will be part of it. Other chapters focus on what it may mean more specifically for politics (3 and 6), energy and resources (3 and 14), work (4), welfare (5 and 16), money (7, 12, and 15), health (9), and various aspects of national and local (and European) policy (11, 13 and 16). The different chapters cross-link with one another in many ways.

The book should interest people, especially younger people, who are professionally or academically involved in the future of society, politics, work, welfare, the monetary and financial system, health, economics, energy, resources and environment, and the other fields it discusses. But I hope it will also interest active citizens not professionally involved in those fields, who are aware of the need for radical change. Their role in helping to bring it about will be crucial. Owing to the pressures of professional groupthink and the over-riding imperatives of career survival and success, most mainstream practitioners in all walks of life—including politics and the communications media—become prisoners of the existing systems of organisation and perception in which they operate, and lose the capacity to do more than tinker with them. Countervailing pressures from active citizens outside are essential to getting important new issues and important new ideas on to mainstream agendas.

THE HISTORICAL CONTEXT

A brief survey of the past twenty years and the next half-century will help to put these lectures and papers in context.

The dominant political rhetoric of the past twenty years, typified by the Thatcherite 1980s, has also professed hostility to 'the culture of dependency'. But, as will be clear, that is not to be confused with the approach to self-reliance developed in this book. That rhetoric was fundamentally dishonest. Those who propagated it gave no serious attention to helping people and nations to become more self-reliant. On the contrary, their rhetoric masked a relentless drive to deepen the dependency of people and nations on big business and big finance, and to establish the supremacy of those institutions through global and national alliances with right-wing governments. The result, as everyone knows, has been greatly to widen the gap in power and wealth between rich and poor people and nations.

The strength of this right-wing revival reflected the strength of the backlash against state socialism and overpowerful labour unions. But, in any more fundamental sense, it was not a radical change. It was just another swing of the pendulum in the struggle between the élites of conventional industrial-age capitalism and conventional industrial-age socialism—their struggle with one another for power over the rest of society. The idea that its global counterpart—the collapse of communism and the Soviet Empire—was 'the end of history'[1] and not just the end of the Cold War, was the reverse of the truth. The truth is that removal of the threat posed by world communism has opened up the possibility of moving forward to a new stage of history, involving the radical transformation of 'free-market' capitalism too. It has created an opportunity to change direction to a people-centred or citizen-centred path of human progress, instead of a business-centred, finance-centred, or state-centred future.[2] It is that opportunity which is the subject matter of this book.

Far from having brought us to the end of history, then, the end of the Cold War confronts us with the need to decide what the next phase of history is to be. As the limits of the Earth's capacity close in, will people's dependency on the remote workings of national and multinational business, finance, government and the communications media grow ever deeper, and the gap between rich and poor, powerful and weak, dominant and dependent, grow ever wider? Or shall we, in order to meet the challenge of a shrinking world, break out of our modern culture of domination and dependency, and break through to a new post-modern culture of greater equality and self-reliance?

COMING CHANGES

The next half-century will see two great changes, one in the structure of world power and the other in the nature of economic progress worldwide. Both underline the urgency of creating a more democratic world order.

As regards the structure of power, the modern period of history has seen Europe and North America dominating the world politically, economically

---

[1] Francis Fukuyama, *The End of History and the Last Man*: Penguin 1992.

[2] Some current mainstream rethinking is beginning to move in this direction. One example is the revival (Will Hutton, *The State We're in*, Vintage, 1996) of the 1970's idea of stakeholder capitalism, with a framework for business 'based quite clearly on the requirement that those in charge shall serve the interests of all the stakeholders—including especially the employees, customers, investors and the public, as well as suppliers and creditors—and maintain a fair balance between them' (James Robertson, *Power, Money & Sex: Towards A New Social Balance*, Marion Boyars, 1976, pp. 52–3). But note that this still assumes an organisation-centred, not a people-centred, economy.

and culturally. In the 21st century that supremacy will decline. The balance of economic power is already shifting. Japan and South East Asia are competitive now. China, India, Indonesia and Brazil soon will be. As time passes, the balance of geopolitical power will shift too.

Britain was world leader in the 19th century, and sterling was the world currency. In the 20th century the USA became world leader, and the US dollar became the world currency. As Euroamerican power declines, what is to replace it? A new version of global domination and dependency under a new superpower—China perhaps—with us Euroamericans taking our turn to be under their thumb? Or can we create a more democratic world order than today's, which will protect us and everyone else more effectively from other people's superior power than the rest of the world has been protected from ours in the last few centuries?[3]

As regards economic progress, in its present form it is in its terminal stage. It is leading to a dead end—all too literally. Already, the present human population is consuming and polluting more than the Earth can sustain. Ultimately world population is likely to double, if not more. That all people on Earth could ever attain the high-consuming, high-polluting ways of life of today's rich countries, is a sheer impossibility. A change of direction to progress of a different kind is bound to come, either through purposeful endeavour or as the aftermath of global catastrophe.

The only way to avoid catastrophe will be for the world community to agree and carry out a global compact on the following lines:

- We who live in the rich North will have to use very much more efficiently than we do now a very much smaller share of the world's natural resources (which we now grossly overuse). That will mean using our 'human resources' (which we now grossly underemploy and underdevelop) very much more efficiently too.
- We will have to persuade—we cannot compel—the 'developing' countries of the South and the countries of the former Soviet bloc that they too should switch to this conserving and enabling development path. The South, in particular, must also be persuaded to limit its population growth. However, we high-consuming, high-polluting people in the North should not suggest that population control in the South is global priority Number One. If we do, we will simply provoke the South to respond that the top priority is for us to limit our

---

[3] Another possibility, at least in the transition period, could be an oligarchic global order, with world leadership divided between a small number of regional blocs such as North America, Europe, and East Asia. But that might turn out to be only a half-way house to world domination by a new superpower.

consumption, pollution and waste, and the argument will get none of us anywhere.

- In our own self-interest, and in view of our heavy share of responsibility for the world's environmental and poverty crisis today, we should do all we can to help the South and the former Soviet bloc countries with this new approach to development.
- To do so effectively, we will have to democratise the institutions of global economic governance—including the World Bank, International Monetary Fund, and the new World Trade Organisation. At present they are neither representative of nor answerable to the great majority of the world's peoples, and do not have their confidence.

Unless we can persuade the other peoples of the world to adopt this new more conserving approach to more self-reliant progress, their further development will put our future in peril as well as their own. In order to persuade them to adopt it we will have to adopt it wholeheartedly ourselves. Doing so will, in fact, help us to solve our own environmental problems and our own problems of unemployment, rising poverty and crime, a growing 'underclass' and declining social cohesion. We will be creating better-quality lives for ourselves and our children; we will be leaving a fairer share of the Earth's natural resources and its capacity to absorb pollution and waste, for use by the peoples of the majority world; and we will be offering them a new model of development, to which we are clearly committed ourselves.

Our future capacity to play an effective role in the world as a whole will therefore depend on our giving top priority to shifting our own countries on to a new path of people-centred and ecologically benign progress. Scientists calculate that the required 'dematerialisation' of our economic lives may involve a reduction of up to 90% in our use of fossil fuels and other materials over the next thirty or forty years. But they also say this is technically feasible, and would improve the quality of life in many respects. The question is about the political will and the public understanding needed to carry it out.

'POST-INDUSTRIAL' AND 'POST-MODERN'

The terms 'post-industrial' and 'post-modern' have already appeared, and will appear again frequently. They call for comment.

First, neither says anything about the new era we are entering. They tell us only that the industrial era or the modern era is ending. However, that this is happening and we are entering a new era is important in itself. Nobody can yet know how the new period of history will be best described. And, in any case, our main concern is to help to shape it, not to predict or describe what it will be like.

Second, the term 'post-industrial' can mean two different things. One, which I prefer to call 'hyper-industrial' or 'hyper-expansionist' (HE), refers to a marked acceleration of industrial-age trends and drives, and a consequent deepening of people's dependency on big organisations, powerful technologies, expert knowledge, and high finance. The other, which I call sane, humane and ecological (SHE), refers to a future in which progress becomes people-centred, as industrial-age trends and drives lose much of their force. As Chapter 2 suggests, the conflict between these two competing visions of post-industrial society can be seen, in terms that Marx might have used had he been living now, as the motor force which is driving the post-modern revolution.

Third, in literature and the arts the term 'post-modern' is mainly used to refer to the breakdown of modern certainties and the onset of chaos and confusion: ' 'T'is all in pieces, all cohesion gone', as John Donne wrote of the collapse of medieval certainties and the birthpangs of modern understanding. But that need not prevent our using 'post-modern' in a more constructive sense. Literature and the arts are about experience and expression—experiencing what is happening and expressing emotional responses to it. The practical response can then follow. For people living through the breakdown of modern ways of living, organising and thinking, the practical response is to help to shape viable post-modern alternatives. As it happens, the social, economic, political and intellectual reconstruction envisaged in the following chapters does, in fact, display some of the qualities of diversity, freedom, equality, democracy and subjectivity which are regarded as characteristic of post-modernism in literature and the arts.

Fourth, 'post-industrial' and 'post-modern' convey different but complementary meanings. 'Post-industrial' focuses attention on changes typical of the ending of the two-hundred-year period of the industrial age, contrasted with the changes that were typical of its beginning and its development. 'Post-modern' focuses attention on the more fundamental changes typical of the ending of the five-hundred-year modern era, as contrasted with the changes typical of its beginning and development.

Readers will notice a tendency to shift from a post-industrial perspective in the earlier chapters to a post-modern perspective in the later ones. This reflects my growing awareness that, as the century and millennium draw to an end, the changes facing the industrialised countries—and all others—can only be understood, not just as a change in the industrial way of life, but as an aspect of wider and more fundamental changes affecting the world as a whole.

As I have said, the material reprinted here is mainly about aspects of the new path of progress as it will affect Britain, Europe and other parts of the North. But the modern culture of domination and dependency has pervaded the whole world. We are all caught up in it together. The same principles—the decolonisation of institutionalised power, and the liberation of people from it to be self-reliant, co-operative and responsible—are valid everywhere, as we seek to negotiate the worldwide post-industrial, post-modern transition.

The Old Bakehouse, Cholsey
January 1997

1

Post-Industrial Liberation

This paper was written for an Acton Society Trust conference organised by Krishan Kumar at Cumberland Lodge, Windsor Great Park, in July 1977. It was given again at a meeting of the British Association for the Advancement of Science on 'Interdisciplinary Research and Social Progress' organised by Steve Cook at Aston University in September 1977. It was published in *New Universities Quarterly*, Winter 1977/78.

Since starting to work as an independent writer and speaker, I had published two short books in Marion Boyars' 'Ideas In Progress' series— *Profit Or People: The New Social Role of Money* (1974) and *Power, Money and Sex: Towards a New Social Balance* (1976). Those were concerned mainly with changes I had learned were needed *within* the systems of finance, government and politics, during my twenty years' work in them. I was aware that this paper for the Acton Society Trust reflected advances in my thinking—the realisation that 'developed' as well as 'developing' countries had an informal sector, that the continuing replacement of informal by formal activities was a significant part of what is conventionally taken to be economic progress, and that the liberation of people from excessive dependency on the institutions of the formal sector would be analogous to the process of decolonisation which had accompanied the last years of the British Empire.

At the end of the paper I acknowledge my debt to Georges Gueron and Gurth Higgin. There were other influences too. The line of thought I was taking was stimulated by reading Ivan Illich's *Celebration of Awareness*, *Tools for Conviviality* and other books; and by my friendship with Peter Cadogan, who argued then—and does so still today—that the 'gift economy' should play a larger part in our lives. The friendships we made with Hazel Henderson and Willis Harman when Alison Pritchard and I did a ten-week journey round the USA and Canada in 1976 still contribute to my thinking on these questions today. To the friendship we made with Bill Dyson of the Vanier Institute of the Family in Ottawa, and his commitment to 'seeing the economy whole', I owed many subsequent discussions in Canada.

January 1997

1

Post-Industrial Liberation and Reconstruction

In this paper I want to explore the hypothesis that industrial society may develop towards the kind of post-industrial society in which people will be less, not more, dependent on money and jobs and public services.

The transition to such a post-industrial society would gather momentum as it became increasingly apparent that the most successful and rewarding way for many people to achieve satisfying material standards of living and a high quality of life was to play a more direct personal part in creating them for themselves and their fellows. This would involve a reversal of the prevailing tendency of industrial societies to institutionalise more and more aspects of production, consumption, caring, teaching, healing, and the other activities of life.

The possibility would arise that de-institutionalisation of economic activity would become a cumulative, self-reinforcing, self-sustaining movement—taking off in much the same kind of way as the industrial revolution took off in 18th- and 19th-century Britain. From one point of view this would be a liberation movement—people liberating themselves and others from dependence on the institutionalised economy. From another point of view it would be a process of voluntary decolonisation—the managers of the institutionalised economy aiming to enable other people to become less and less dependent on it. From a third point of view it would be a process of metaphysical reconstruction,[1] involving a revision of industrial/institutional concepts of work, wealth, and welfare. From all three points of view practical and conceptual questions would arise with which the social sciences, and especially economics, might find it hard to come to terms.

THE DUAL ECONOMY

The economy is in two parts—the institutionalised part and the informal part.

The institutionalised part of the economy is the part in which people

---

[1] I owe this term to E. F. Schumacher, *Small Is Beautiful: Economics as if People Mattered*, Blond and Briggs, 1973.

work for money in jobs generated by the labour market; the goods they make and the services they provide are purchased for money or otherwise financed, for example by taxation. This part of the economy consists of the primary (farming, forestry, mining) sector, the secondary (manufacturing) sector, and the tertiary and quaternary (services and service-to-services) sectors. The informal part of the economy consists of the domestic (household) sector and the marginal (community) sector. In this part of the economy the labour market does not operate (people don't have jobs), work is mainly unpaid (like housework), and goods and services are mainly given away or exchanged. The informal part of the economy is sometimes described as the gift and barter economy, as opposed to the money economy, though it also includes many unrecorded cash transactions.

Everyone lives, to a greater or lesser extent, in both parts of the dual economy. But in industrialised societies attention is concentrated on the institutional part of the economy, the part in which business corporations, government agencies and other organisations operate and in which individuals make and spend money. The prevailing concept of wealth is of something created in the institutionalised part of the economy by the 'economic' activities of industry and commerce and then spent, partly on the consumption of goods and services which people purchase from industry and commerce, and partly on the provision of 'social' well-being by public services. These public services are financed as a spin-off from the economic activities of industry and commerce, which are therefore seen as the 'wealth-creating' activities of society.

In all industrial countries there are important differences of opinion—between conservatives and liberals, between capitalists and socialists, between spokesmen for business, finance, and trade unions, and among politicians, government officials, commentators in the news media, private lobbies and public interest groups—about how the economy should work, and about what changes should be made in various aspects of it. But the prevailing assumption in industrial society is that the production of economic goods and the provision of social services by the institutionalised sectors are the only kinds of economic production and social provision that really matter. Economists and statisticians, politicians and civil servants, trade unionists and bankers, are concerned only with the kind of goods and services which cost money and with the kind of work which is done for an employer for money—jobs in the so-called labour market. Work which is done in the household or marginal sectors, such as housework, does not count in the employment statistics; and goods which are produced there, such as fruit and vegetables grown in gardens and allotments, do not count in the Gross National Product (GNP).

4

The thrust of industrialisation, and the momentum it has developed in the past 200 years, has driven people increasingly out of the informal part of the economy into the institutionalised part. The pressure continues today. For example, single-parent mothers and fathers are encouraged to go out of their homes into jobs in the labour market, thus making the children dependent on institutionalised child care services. In general, men, women and children alike are encouraged to look outside the home for work, for the physical necessities of life, for teaching, for care, for entertainment. The process has been self-reinforcing, like the drift from public transport to private transport. As economic activity has shifted away from the home and local community, the home and local community have become less and less able to meet the economic and social needs of the people who still remain there, thus pushing them also into the money economy and the labour market. This is a prime example of 'the tyranny of small decisions'.[2] The large decision—whether people would be better off if we generally lived a greater proportion of our lives in the informal economy—is pre-empted by the multitude of small choices which present themselves to us as the economy becomes more and more institutionalised.

LIMITS TO THE INSTITUTIONALISED ECONOMY

However, there is mounting evidence that limits may now be closing in on the institutionalised economy. We may classify these limits under four different headings: social scarcity; psychological remoteness; institutional congestion; conceptual disarray. I will touch on them very briefly.

SOCIAL SCARCITY. As Fred Hirsch has pointed out in *Social Limits To Growth*,[3] the growth of the institutionalised economy tends to decrease the value of socially scarce goods once they are attained. He cites traffic congestion and higher education as examples. The satisfaction derived from an automobile depends on the traffic conditions in which it can be used, and these will deteriorate as use becomes more widespread. The value of higher education, as a launching pad for a good job, is inversely related to the number of people who have also had access to it. As access to higher education spreads, therefore, its 'positional' value declines. Hirsch contrasts the positional economy with the material economy, and defines the former as covering everything that is either scarce in itself or subject to congestion by extensive

[2] See Fred Hirsch, *Social Limits to Growth*, Routledge and Kegan Paul, 1977, p. 168.
[3] Ibid., p. 66.

5

use; and he points out that:

> As general standards of living rise...competition moves increasingly from the material sector to the positional sector, where what one wins another loses in a zero-sum game. As the frontier closes, positional competition intensifies...In the positional sector, individuals chase each other's tails. The race gets longer for the same prize.

In other words, many of the goods delivered by the institutionalised economy become progressively less valuable as it grows. Eventually a limit is reached. The advanced industrial countries are not far off it now, in many respects.

PSYCHOLOGICAL REMOTENESS. As more and more people in an industrialised society come to depend for more and more aspects of their life on the institutionalised economy rather than on the household and local community, their sense of alienation and dependence grows greater. They therefore feel entitled—indeed, compelled—to make greater and greater demands for jobs, for pay, for goods and commercial services, and for public and social services. Sooner or later the time is bound to come when these demands will outrun the economy's capacity to meet them, and at this point rising unemployment (too big a demand for jobs) and rising inflation (too big a demand for money) become systemic. Peter Jay described this situation last year as 'the contradiction of existing political economy' in a published paper on 'a general hypothesis of employment, inflation, and politics'.[4] He reached:

> the depressing conclusion that the operation of free democracy appears to force governments into positions (the commitment to full employment) which prevent them from taking the steps (fiscal and monetary restraint) which are necessary to arrest the menace (accelerating inflation) that threatens to undermine the condition (stable prosperity) on which political stability and therefore liberal democracy depend. In other words, democracy has itself by the tail and is eating itself up fast.

INSTITUTIONAL CONGESTION. As the institutionalised economy developed, it inevitably became increasingly complex and congested. It has now reached the point where the supposedly wealth-creating activities of industry and commerce are generating such great social costs, and the interrelations between industry, finance, government, trade unions, and the public services have become so intertwined, that the workings of the system are grinding towards a halt. The American economist, Hazel Henderson, describes this as

[4] Peter Jay, *Employment, Inflation and Politics*, Institute of Economic Affairs, London, 1976.

'the entropy state' which, she says:

> is a society at the stage when complexity and interdependence have reached such unmodelable, unmanageable proportions that the transaction costs generated equal or exceed its productive capabilities. In a manner analogous to physical systems, the society winds down of its own weight and the proportion of its gross national product that must be spent in mediating conflicts, controlling crime, footing the bill for all the social costs generated by the externalities of production and consumption, providing ever more comprehensive bureaucratic co-ordination, and generally trying to maintain 'social homeostasis', begins to grow exponentially or even hyper-exponentially. Such societies may have already drifted to a soft-landing in a steady state, with inflation masking their declining condition.[5]

CONCEPTUAL DISARRAY. The conventional 'economic/institutional' paradigm is beginning to lose credibility.

First, the idea that economic wealth must be created by industry and commerce before it can be spent on the provision of social well-being by the public services is wearing thin. Increasingly, people are asking why it should be necessary, for example, to build and sell more automobiles in order to be able to afford more schools and teachers; or why it should be necessary to make and sell more cigarettes and sweets in order to be able to afford more doctors and dentists. What sort of 'wealth' is this, which is created and consumed in this way? Second, the idea that wealth is created in the formal sector of the economy but not in the informal sector—that the economic production of the country actually goes down if people grow their own vegetables instead of buying them in the shops—is also wearing thin.

The following two quotations illustrate the two growing areas of doubt:

> To the indiscriminate growth economists it doesn't matter whether the products of industrial activity are more sweets to rot the children's teeth, or insulating blocks for houses. Essentially, the concern is with measured economic busyness rather than with purposes.[6]

> How easily we could turn the tables on the economists if we all decided that from tomorrow morning, the work of the domestic economy should be paid for. Instead of cooking dinner for her own lot, each housewife would feed her neighbors at regular restaurant rates; then they'd cook for her family and get their money back. We'd do each other's housework and gardening at award rates. Big money would change hands when we fixed each other's tap washers and electric plugs at the plumbers' and electricians' rates. Without a scrap of extra

[5] Hazel Henderson, *The Coming Economic Transition*, Princeton Center for Alternative Futures, 1976.

[6] Peter Draper, *Economic Policy and Health*, Unit for the Study of Health Policy, London, 1976.

work Gross National Product (GNP) would go up by a third overnight. We would increase that to half if the children rented each other's back yards and paid each other as play supervisors, and we could double it if we all went to bed next door at regular massage parlor rates. Our economists would immediately be eager to find out what line of investment was showing such fabulous growth in capital/output ratio. They'd find that housing was bettered only by double beds and they'd recommend a massive switch of investment into both. Don't laugh, because in reverse, this nonsense measures exactly the distortion we get in our national accounts now.[7]

Economists are, in fact, increasingly beginning to claim that GNP has never purported to measure the use value of economic activity; they have always recognised that it simply represents the exchange value of all goods and services produced in the money economy; it does not differentiate between desirable and undesirable economic activity; nor does it differentiate between final economic consumption and intermediate economic activity which is under-taken to treat disease, clean up pollution, salvage accidents and mitigate damage caused by other economic activities. Some analysts are actually now suggesting that rising GNP in industrialised countries today probably measures mainly the rising costs of pollution, environmental degradation and human suffering; and, although that cannot be proved, it is a further indication of the declining credibility of rising GNP either as a measure of economic well-being or as a desirable goal of economic endeavour.[8]

THE FUTURE

A brief look at future possibilities will be helpful here.

The direction in which the economies of today's industrialised countries will develop during the next three or four decades can be envisaged as a mix between three possible futures or scenarios. Any one of these might prove dominant to a greater or lesser extent. The balance between them will change over time. They are: the industrial future; the hyper-industrial future; and the post-industrial future.[9]

[7] Hugh Stretton, *Housing and Government*, Australian Broadcasting Commision, Sydney, 1974.

[8] [1997 note. This has now been well documented, for example for the United States in the Index of Sustainable Economic Welfare in the Appendix to Herman Daly and John Cobb, *For the Common Good, Redirecting the Economy towards Community, the Environment and a Sustainable Future*, Greenprint, 1990 and for Britain in Tim Jackson and Nic Marks, *Measuring Sustainable Economic Welfare*, New Economics Foundation, 1994.]

[9] [1997 footnote. By 1978—see Chapter 2—I had renamed these Business-As-Usual, Hyper-Expansionist (HE) and Sane, Humane and Ecological (SHE).]

INDUSTRIAL FUTURE. This would be one in which the mainspring of economic activity continued to be manufacturing industry. Industrial assumptions would continue dominant: wealth is created by the production and sale of material goods; wealth is consumed in the form of services and amenities, as well as material goods; the availability of good health, good education, and other forms of social well-being, thus depends on the continued prosperity of manufacturing industries like automobiles, chemicals and engineering; and the top priorities will continue to be industrial productivity and economic growth.

The industrial future represents a business-as-usual scenario. It implies that the problems of reconciling (a) high levels of industrial investment; (b) high levels of employment; and (c) the social and environmental impacts of industrialisation will continue to be important. It therefore implies a continuing high level of economic intervention by governments to control inflation and unemployment, to enforce pollution control, to provide social welfare, to give equal opportunities to minority groups, and so on. It implies a continuing distinction between the economic and social aspects of life, and between work and leisure. It implies that the 'work ethic' will remain strong, in the conventional sense that most people will continue to regard a job as a necessary prerequisite for status and self-esteem.

The strongest factor in favour of the industrial scenario is that the continuing momentum of existing trends and conventional economic aspirations is bound to influence the future very considerably. The doubt about it has already been pointed out. Evidence is accumulating that limits inherent in the economic/institutional paradigm may be beginning to close in.

HYPER-INDUSTRIAL FUTURE. This view of the future resembles the industrial view in many ways, but holds that the industrialised economies are now going through a significant shift of emphasis from traditional manufacturing industries to advanced technologies and knowledge-based service industries, which will open up new possibilities for expansion. Exponents of the hyper-industrial view[10] include Herman Kahn,[11] Daniel Bell[12] and Peter Drucker.[13]

The hyper-industrial future is seen as a logical extension of the industrial past. Just as the economies of today's industrial countries progressed

---

[10] Advocates of the hyper-industrial view often call it 'post-industrial', which is confusing.

[11] Herman Kahn, *The Next 200 Years*, Associated Business Programmes, London, 1976.

[12] Daniel Bell, *The Coming of Post-Industrial Society: A Venture in Social Forecasting*, Basic Books, New York, 1973.

[13] Peter F. Drucker, *The Age of Discontinuity*, Harper and Row, New York, 1969.

historically from the primary commodity stage to the secondary manufacturing stage, so now they are progressing through the tertiary service stage towards the quaternary service-to-service stage. Among the growing points in an economy of this kind are universities, research institutes and consultancies, and industries like aerospace, telecommunications and computing. All these provide services to sectors like transport, communications and finance, which themselves provide services to corporations and individuals. Shifting the emphasis into these knowledge-based, high technology industries and services will, according to this scenario, enable today's industrial countries to retain their markets in the developing countries as the latter enter fully on the industrial manufacturing stage.

The hyper-industrial scenario shares the underlying assumptions of the industrial scenario, that 'wealth' is created by the provision and sale of goods and services which other people and other countries will be willing to buy, and that expansion can continue indefinitely. The prospect of space colonisation is an important element in it. So is the further development of nuclear power as an energy source. The hyper-industrial scenario shares the industrial scenario's assumption that the economic relationship between the industrialised and developing countries will continue to be asymmetrical, with the former continuing to lead the latter along the path of economic progress. But the hyper-industrial scenario is more challenging than the industrial scenario. It holds that the future for today's industrialised countries lies in accelerating the shift from conventional manufacturing industry to the high technology, know-how, and professional service industries; and that the underlying task of the business system (and for public policy) in those countries is to manage this transition successfully.

There are powerful factors in favour of this scenario, including the widespread assumption that progress is to do with increasing technical sophistication and the extrapolation of existing trends. But it also raises technical, political, psychological and conceptual difficulties. The feasibility of widespread automation, space colonisation, and massive nuclear power programmes in the next few decades remains in doubt. When the basic needs of billions of Third World people are not yet met, would it be possible for the industrialised countries to concentrate on creating a high technology future for themselves? Transitional unemployment in the industrialised countries might be unacceptably high; and, once the technocratic, automated hyper-industrial economy were achieved, would it be able to satisfy the higher level needs of the leisured irresponsible masses for self-esteem and self-actualisation? Finally, how would the hyper-industrial (hyper-institutionalised) economy be able to break out of the limits that (as we have seen) may now be closing in on the institutionalised economy?

POST-INDUSTRIAL FUTURE. Thus we have to envisage the possibility of an economic future not subject to the infeasibilities which might invalidate the industrial and hyper-industrial scenarios. This would be the post-industrial future. The post-industrial economy would differ from the industrial and hyper-industrial economies in two fundamental features. First, its underlying principle would be equilibrium not expansion. Second, it would involve the de-institutionalisation of economic activity, not its further institutionalisation. These two features would be closely related.

This paper is not concerned to evaluate the probability of a post-industrial future; nor to discuss the operating characteristics of an equilibrium economy, as such. My purpose is restricted to considering certain aspects of the de-institutionalisation of economic activity that would be part of the transition to a post-industrial, equilibrium economy, if that transition occurred. These can be outlined under three headings: liberation; decolonisation; and metaphysical reconstruction.

LIBERATION

The following speculations will serve to indicate some of the questions that may arise.

People can liberate themselves—to a greater or lesser extent—from the institutionalised economy, and develop alternatives to it. They can decide to do more of their work and more of their living in and around their households and local communities—to create use value rather than exchange value by their work. As more and more people decide to do this, they may become part of a widespread movement towards greater economic self-reliance, alternative technologies, alternative health, rural resettlement, and so forth. Many people in countries like Britain and the United States are already doing these things.

If this liberation movement continued to grow, it might well come to be seen as the post-industrial counterpart to the industrial revolution which occurred in Britain in the late 18th and early 19th centuries. As a starting hypothesis, we may postulate that this post-industrial revolution would be predominantly social and psychological in character, whereas the industrial revolution was predominantly technical and economic. On that basis, it is instructive to examine some possible parallels with the industrial revolution relying on Peter Mathias's book *The First Industrial Nation*[14] as a pointer to some of its main characteristics.

One of the main prerequisites for the industrial revolution was the

[14] Peter Mathias, *The First Industrial Revolution*, Methuen, 1969.

11

existence of sufficient economic resources to develop new dimensions to the economy. In 18th century Britain plentiful coal and iron were conveniently placed for water transport in many parts of the country, and a strategic river system, based on the rivers Trent and Severn, stretched into the heart of industrial England. A corresponding prerequisite for the post-industrial revolution would be the existence of sufficient social and psychological resources to develop new social and psychological dimensions to our economic and political lives. These social and psychological resources could include: large numbers of active people leisured or unemployed; large numbers of active people socially and psychologically aware; a widespread understanding that psychological and social drives now provide the leading edge of change—not economic and commercial drives; and the existence of systems of education, information and communication not wholly closed to new ideas, not wholly mesmerised by conventional fashion, and not wholly dominated by economic and political forces committed to the *status quo*.

Another factor in the industrial revolution was inventiveness, a readiness to use other people's ideas and skills, and the capacity to generate an increasing flow of technical innovations through which physical production and economic productivity could be increased. The post-industrial revolution would also need inventiveness—to generate an increasing flow of social innovations through which the social and psychological equivalents of production and productivity can be increased.

Again, a new breed of entrepreneurs played a special part in the energetic experimentation and technical innovation which marked the industrial revolution. These were the men, to quote Mathias:

> under whose charge new sectors of the economy could be developed and new inventions brought into productive use. Such men were the shock troops of economic change.

Who would be the entrepreneurs of social change today, who would facilitate new types of social activity and help to bring social innovations into widespread use? What sort of people would they be; and where would they be found?

Innovation in industry in 18th-century Britain also required the investment of financial capital in the productive process. New channels had to be created, through which money could flow to the people who wanted to use it from the people who had savings (i.e. surplus money) to invest. In due course there developed a linked national network of financial institutions, including the country banks, and the bankers, billbrokers and other specialist intermediaries in the City of London, to handle the transfer of credit from one part of the country to another; and the habit of productive financial investment became established. What would be the post-industrial counterparts to financial capital, to the banking networks, and to the habit of productive investment? Instead of money, perhaps we would mainly be concerned with psychological and social energy. There are many people now who wish to invest their surplus psychological and social energy in other people's projects. They want to receive a psychological, rather than a commercial return on their investment. What new channels and networks would come into existence to link them with the social entrepreneurs and social innovators—the shock troops of social change—who need their backing?

The industrial revolution was a process of industrial innovation which became cumulative and self-sustaining. It was centred upon what Mathias calls the 'new matrix of industries, materials and skills', in which steam power, coal, iron machinery, and engineering skills played the dominant part. This new matrix gave increasing freedom from the old traditional limitations of nature, which had held back economic activity in all previous ages. How would the post-industrial revolution similarly become a self-sustaining process? What new matrix of psycho-social resources, techniques and skills corresponding to Mathias's matrix of industries, materials and engineering skills, would give increasing freedom from the limitations of personal and institutional behaviour which have held back psychological and social growth hitherto, and from the limitations now closing in on the institutionalised economy?

These are the kinds of questions that could have practical relevance for the future. Would they be susceptible to economic analysis? Or is it part of their essence that they would not?

DECOLONISATION

If the development of alternative forms of economic activity by people outside the economic institutions can be seen as a process of liberation, the de-institutionalisation of economic activity by people within the institutions can be seen as a process of decolonisation. According to this view, the constructive task for people who work in government, business, finance, trade unions, public services, the professions and other areas of the institutionalised economy would be to reduce the dependence of other people upon it—that is, to reduce people's dependence on jobs, on money and on goods and services provided by industry, commerce and the public services. The aim would be to enable people—as citizens, customers, workers, patients, pupils, and so on—to develop their own autonomy. The aim of managers, professionals, public servants, and so on, should be to work themselves out of a job—to make themselves redundant.

There is, in fact, some evidence already that professional and managerial people are increasingly trying to develop an enabling role, in which they help their clients to become less dependent on them. For example, I quote the following views expressed in a conference held three years ago in Ottawa on 'The Serving Professions?':

> Professionals should share rather than monopolise their privileged knowledge, give people a chance to learn while they are healing…If poverty is basically the absence of power, social action must involve giving people part of this power back. We lawyers should be training people to understand the law and apply it to represent themselves…The question we must seriously ask ourselves is to what extent are we as physicians prepared to disappear? What we should be asking in our relationships with patients is 'What have I done so this person can manage to do without me in the future?'…Among the social pitfalls fostered by the professions is the trend towards overdependency which verges on helplessness. Among the questions we professionals must ask ourselves is whether we are helpers or hinderers. Are we creating an endless production of services that draw us further into a trap? Do we, through the framing of laws and other structures create barriers that we then must spend valuable time breaking down again?

Other specific examples of this idea that the managerial and professional role is to help people to help themselves—that managers and professionals should give away their powers and teach others to use them, rather than to monopolise them and hire them out—could be quoted from fields ranging from psychoanalysis through banking to environmental planning.

Let us consider briefly what this 'enabling' approach might imply for business and government. Take the oil companies as an example. Oil companies conventionally aim to sell increasing quantities of oil. We envisage the possibility that they would aim to help their customers to buy less oil, by reducing their dependence on it. In other words, the nature of the business would change from producing and selling oil, to helping people to meet their energy needs more independently. Similarly, pharmaceutical and food manufacturing firms conventionally aim to sell increasing quantities of drugs and convenience foods. We envisage that they would be helping their customers to reduce their dependence on these products. The nature of the business would then have changed from producing and selling health products and food products, to helping people to meet their own health needs and food needs in a more self-reliant way.

So far as governments are concerned, instead of continuing to build up capital-intensive industry, centralised energy systems, and bureaucratic public services—and increasing people's dependence upon them for their work, for their material needs and for their social well-being—governments would shift the emphasis to policies which helped people to become more self-sufficient and autonomous. For example:

- Support for decentralised energy production and conservation.
- Job creation programmes, started as a centralised policy for providing more jobs, but subsequently used to prime the economic pump at the local community level.
- Investment in housing and other local facilities (including gardens, workshops, etc.) which would help to develop the economic and social self-reliance of households and local communities.
- Research and development support for a wide range of advanced, small-scale technologies which would also contribute to the economic and social self-reliance of households and local communities.
- Support for rural resettlement, small-scale agriculture, and part-time farming.

Similarly, we could envisage the possibility that financial institutions (like banks) might aim to help people to be less dependent on money, and that trade unions might aim to help people to be less dependent on jobs. In all these cases the same question arises: would enabling, decolonising decisions and policies of this kind on the part of business, government, and other economic institutions be susceptible to economic analysis? Or is it part of their essence that they would not? There would certainly be a problem of how to justify such policies with reference to the kind of criteria with which economic institutions are familiar today. For example, suppose that a government decided to invest public money in a housing programme providing garden and workshop facilities. The aim would be to enable the occupants to become significantly less dependent on the shops for much of their food and many of their household items, and significantly less dependent on the labour market for their work. In other words, the government would be helping people to liberate themselves, at least to some extent, from dependence on the money economy. The problem is: not only would the direct financial return on the investment be 'uneconomic' (according to conventional criteria about rates of return), but the investment would actually reduce the level of measured GNP. So, although a housing policy of this kind might be very successful and valuable in social and human (and real economic) terms, it would be quite unjustifiable according to conventional economic criteria. There would be a multitude of similar cases, for example in spheres such as education and health, where enabling policies would seem to run counter to the conventional economic criteria used to evaluate new proposals today.

15

METAPHYSICAL RECONSTRUCTION

Here are two examples of the kind of reconceptualisation that might take place, in the course of transition to a post-industrial economy:

Wealth. The new wealth might count as affluent the person who possessed the necessary equipment to make the best use of natural energy flows to heat a home or warm water—the use which accounts for the bulk of an individual's energy demand. The symbols of this kind of wealth would not be new cars, TVs or whatever, although they would be just as tangible and just as visible. They would be solar panels, insulated walls or a heat pump. The poor would be those who remained dependent on centralised energy distribution services, vulnerable to interruption by strike, malfunction or sabotage, and even more vulnerable to rising tariffs set by inaccessible technocrats themselves the victims of market forces beyond their control. The new rich would boast not of how new their television was but of how long it was expected to last and how easy it would be to repair. Wealth might take the form of ownership of, or at least access to, enough land to grow a proportion of one's food. This would reduce the need to earn an ever larger income in order to pay for increasingly expensive food. Wealth would consist in having access to most goods and services within easy walking or cycling distance of home, thus reducing the need to spend more time earning more money to pay for more expensive transport services. A high income would be less a sign of wealth than of poverty since it would indicate dependence on the provision by someone else of a job and a workplace in order to earn the income to rent services. Wealth would consist in having more control over the decisions that affected well-being and in having the time to exercise that control.[15]

Work. The enormous intellectual and social ferment of our own times (whether we label it as future shock, or the transition to post-industrial society, the emergence of Consciousness III or the stable state, or childhood's end) is the context for changing concepts of work. Changing concepts of work, whether at the personal or at the community or social level or both, are inescapably related to a changing sense of purpose—of what it is useful to do. The labour market cannot much longer elicit credibility as an organising device for the activity of working. The concept of work as something that must be socially productive in the

[15] Tom Burke, *The New Wealth*, unpublished paper, 1977.

eyes of the beholder is coming to be used to sort meaningful from empty jobs. A whole new concept of work is emerging which will dismiss as work much which now passes for it and will embrace as work much which is not now included in it. We are going to need to rely increasingly on individuals and communities to define their own concepts of work.[16]

In both these cases of wealth and work—and the same applies *mutatis mutandis* to others like welfare and power—the essence of the new concepts would be that it was good to exercise personal control over economic decisions affecting one's own life and to be able to make those decisions according to one's own personal values; and that the desirable economy and society was one in which other people as well as oneself were doing the same. These new concepts would, at the least, call in question how far economic criteria could be applied which purported to be generally valid for everyone— for example, 'measurement of economic welfare' (MEW) statistics, based on consumption rather than production. More generally, they would call in question the opinion of leading economists like Jan Tinbergen that

> progress in our understanding can only be based on the push for measurement of phenomena previously thought to be non-measurable.[17]

It is doubtful if the development of any socioeconomic calculi (whether based on an integration of economic choice theory, political decision theory and game theory, or on a Gross National Happiness index derived from opinion surveys) could be relevant in a situation whose essence was recognised as consisting of a multitudinous plurality of separate value systems.

ACTION LEARNING AS THE NEW ECONOMICS?

The dichotomy between the two parts of the dual economy is, in fact, paralleled in other fields. In each case there are two different forms of activity, as in the dual economy. One is structured, quantitative and institutional; the other is unstructured, qualitative and personal. Thus we have:

- the institutionalised economy *and* the informal economy;
- scientific knowledge *and* intuitive understanding;
- representative government *and* community politics;

---

[16] Gail Stewart and Cathy Starr, *Reworking The World: A Report on Changing Concepts of Work*, Ottawa, 1973.

[17] Kurt Dopfer (ed.), *Economics In The Future*, p. 46, Macmillan, 1976.

- organised religious activity *and* personal spiritual experience; and
- an arm's length relationship (between professional and client) *and* personally shared experience.

The possible reversal of the present imbalance between the institutional and the informal parts of the dual economy is paralleled in these other fields. In all of them the same kinds of questions are arising. These questions are about domination and liberation, about rigidity and creativity, about the overdevelopment of old structures and the upsurge of new aspirations, and about how to reconcile the two opposed forms of activity. Both forms seem to be valid. Yet, as the eminent religious thinker Raimundo Pannikar has put it:

> Applying logos to the myth, amounts to killing the myth: it is like looking for darkness with a torch.[18]

Applying laboratory tests to spiritual healing, bureaucratic scrutiny to community self-help, or economic analysis to social innovation, may destroy the conditions in which spiritual healing, community self-help, or social innovation may take place—like looking for darkness with a torch. More generally, an over-emphasis on the structured, institutional and scientific tends to suppress the capability for unstructured, personal, intuitive action and understanding.

The real nature of the questions that could be arising in this situation for the economic and social sciences is suggested in the following remarks about the exploration of consciousness in Willis Harman's recent book, *An Incomplete Guide to the Future*.[19] Harman says:

> Essentially there are two quite different forms of knowing, and we all use both daily. One form is knowing about things in the manner of scientific facts; it is based on rational and empirical processes. The other form is knowing by intuitive identification with, as in knowing another person; it is based to a considerable extent in unconscious processes...Both kinds of knowledge are subject to the possibility of error. The scientific way of 'knowing about' involves meticulous testing to insure that what is claimed as fact can be validated by other scientists making similar experiments or explorations. But 'intuitive knowing' also demands careful testing to prevent self-deception...In opening up the exploration of consciousness, scientists are forced to confront questions that, throughout most of the history of scientific activity, they have managed to set aside for the philosophers to puzzle over. What are the essential limitations of 'knowledge about', or factual knowledge? What are the ultimate capabilities of

[18] Raimundo Pannikar, *Myth in Religious Phenomenology*, Monchanin, Montreal, June/December, 1976.

[19] Willis W. Harman, *An Incomplete Guide to the Future*, Stanford Alumni Association, California, 1976.

the mind as an observing instrument in discerning intuitive knowledge of the universe and of the mind itself? What are the ways in which intuitive knowledge is best shared and validated?

The new questions arising now for economists include the counterparts of those: What are the essential limitations of formal economics? What are the capabilities of formal economics for understanding (and contributing to the success of) informal economic activity? What are the ways in which choices (including 'resource allocation') can be validated and actions and experiences (including 'production' and 'consumption') can be valued, in the informal economy? In the nature of the case the answers to these questions will not be formulated in advance or from outside by economic theorists. They will only be learned by personal practical experience in the informal economy. Is that where the new frontier for economics will be found? Make room for the barefoot economist.

ACKNOWLEDGMENTS

I am grateful to M. Georges Gueron of the International Foundation for Social Innovation in Paris, and to Professor Gurth Higgin[20] of Loughborough University of Technology, for recent opportunities to work on some of the ideas in this paper.

7 St Ann's Villas, London
1977

---

[20] [1997 footnote. Gurth Higgin's *Symptoms Of Tomorrow*, Plume Press/Ward Lock, London, 1973, is a book which did not attract the attention it should have done. I greatly admired it and learned much from it in the later 1970s.]

19

2

A Post-Marxist Strategy

The paper reprinted in this chapter was given at a session on 'Responsibility and Response-ability' at a national conference on 'Shaping The Future: Canada in a Global Society' at the University of Ottawa in August 1978. It was published in the Conference Proceedings, edited by Walter Baker, Centre for Policy and Management Studies, Ottawa.

It takes forward the ideas in Chapter 1, as subsequently developed in *The Sane Alternative*. After referring to the two contrasting visions of a post-industrial future outlined there, Hyper-Expansionist (HE) and Sane, Humane, Ecological (SHE), it gives particular attention to the SHE alternative, analyses the nature of the new direction of progress it will involve, and discusses the strategy needed to bring that change of direction about.

The late 1970s was an exciting time, when many people's ideas about 'alternatives' were developing rapidly. This chapter reflects an advance on the thinking in Chapter 1 in the following respects:

- the idea that conflict in late industrial society would increasingly tend to polarise around the two visions of post-industrial society;
- the idea that, in Marxist terms, that conflict could become the 'motor force' driving a post-industrial (as contrasted with a proletarian) revolution; and
- the idea that the strategy appropriate to a peaceful post-industrial revolution could be defined by contrast with the Marxist strategy for a proletarian revolution.

January 1997

A Post-Marxist Strategy for the Post-Industrial Revolution

> At the genesis of all revolutionary action lies an act of faith: the certainty that the world can be transformed, that man has the power to create something new, and that each of us is personally responsible for this transformation.

This quotation from Roger Garaudy's book, *The Alternative Future*, provides an apt keynote for what I have to say. In asking me to give a paper on 'Responsibility and Response-ability', the organisers of this conference had in mind that I would discuss 'individual responsibility and the human and institutional constraints to moral initiative' in the broad context of 'Culture, Society and the Individual'. I shall address this question in the context of a revolutionary situation. The revolution in question is the post-industrial revolution. Responsibility concerns what we ought to do, and response-ability what we are able to do, to help to bring this revolution about.

One of the most pressing problems today for many people in countries like ours is that they do not like the way things are going and know that a better alternative must be possible, but they do not see how they can help to bring it about. They feel helpless as individuals. They get no constructive vision or sense of purposeful solidarity from their institutions—political parties, churches, and so on. They feel imprisoned and immobilised by their own selves—by their habits, their personality, and the knowledge of their own past ineffectiveness. They also feel imprisoned and immobilised by their institutions; they dare not rebel against the firm on which they depend for their job and their pension, the mortgage company on which they depend for their house, the utilities on which they depend for necessities like heat and light, and the medical and social services on which they depend for their welfare.

Discussion of what to do often revolves around the dilemma: should we first try to change society, or ourselves? Politicians and economists are among those who tend to assume that we should concentrate on changing the structure of society—either by reform or revolution—in order to create the kind of environment in which people can live better lives. Priests and psychiatrists, whose concern is directly with people, are among those who tend to assume that we should concentrate on changing ourselves, since otherwise we shall be incapable of creating a better society. The fact is, of

23

course, that the dilemma is total. Which comes first, the chicken or the egg?

This, then, is my starting point. Each of the ways in which people traditionally strive to create a better world—economic and social reform, political revolution, and personal change—is doomed to failure unless we pursue all three simultaneously. So far as reform is concerned, I have described elsewhere[1] how the 'institutional imperative' ensures that all reform will be too little and too late. Another British thinker, Ronald Higgins,[2] also with personal experience of high level government, has recently concluded that the frightening inertia of our political institutions is one of the main factors leading us into a world of rapidly mounting confusion and horror. But political revolution is no answer either; it merely substitutes one set of rulers—one form of domination—for another, and otherwise leaves things much as they were or worse. Finally, concentration on personal change is all too often tantamount to dropping out, turning one's back on the world in order to take care of oneself. Those who commit themselves to economic and social reform, or to political revolution, or to personal change, as *the* answer, may find self-importance, self-expression and self-satisfaction in so doing. But it is self-delusion for them to suppose, in the face of all evidence, that they will thereby create a better world.

The realistic approach is to seek to change society and ourselves at the same time, by the same actions. The search is for ways in which people can simultaneously change the direction of their personal lives, contribute to reforming the institutional structure of society, and help to bring about a post-industrial revolution which will create a better society. My aim in this paper is to suggest what this will involve.

The approach is a personal one. It is practical, not academic. I shall outline the future that I hope to help create, and suggest ways in which we can help to create it. Up to this point I shall be drawing on the themes of *The Sane Alternative*.[3] But then I shall break new ground and, in the last main section of the paper, I will try to show that my approach, though not Marxist, takes account of Marxism in certain significant respects.

This is important. Our vision of the future is post-industrial, not pre-industrial; it builds on and goes beyond the technical progress made since the Industrial Revolution. It is post-modern, not pre-modern; it builds on and goes beyond the economic and cultural progress made since the Renaissance. It is post-Christian, not pre-Christian; it builds on and goes beyond the

[1] James Robertson, *Power, Money and Sex: Towards a New Social Balance*, Marion Boyars, 1976.
[2] Ronald Higgins, *The Seventh Enemy: The Human Factor in the Global Crisis*, Hodder and Stroughton, 1978.
[3] James Robertson, *The Sane Alternative: Signposts to a Self-Fulfilling Future*, Robertson, 1978. [1997 footnote. In the revised 1983 edition the subtitle became *A Choice of Futures*.]

spiritual progress made in the Christian era. Similarly, our perception of how the post-industrial revolution will take place must build on the insights about the dynamics of social change which Karl Marx and his followers have given to us, and go beyond them. It must be post-Marxist, not pre-Marxist.

OUTLINES OF A NEW FUTURE

The industrial age is ending. Although many people still find it difficult to imagine anything other than a Business-As-Usual future, such a future is not feasible for the industrialised countries or the world as a whole. Limits— physical, social, psychological, institutional, conceptual—are closing in. Britain, the first industrial country, is among the first to hit these limits. In other countries of Europe and North America industrialism may have a few more years to go, but not very many. So what sort of post-industrial society do we want?

Leaving aside the possibilities of Disaster and Totalitarian Clampdown (both of which have their prophets), there are two sharply contrasting views of post-industrial society. I refer to them as the Hyper-Expansionist (HE) future and the Sane, Humane, Ecological (SHE) future. The second is the kind of post-industrial society I want to help to create. I shall briefly describe it: first by contrasting it with the HE future; second, by suggesting some of the changes it would involve.

A HYPER-EXPANSION (HE) FUTURE

The HE view of the future has been expounded by North American thinkers like Herman Kahn and Daniel Bell. They assume that the post-industrial revolution will be a transition to a super-industrial way of life. High technology industries like aerospace, computing and telecommunications will set the pace, supported by the knowledge-based, information-handling professions and occupations. The service industries will continue to overtake manufacturing as the growth points of the economy. Personal and social services, including the provision of care, amenities and entertainment, will continue to become more institutionalised and professionalised. By accelerating these existing trends in modern society—and by relying on advanced science and technology in areas like space colonisation, nuclear energy, automation, genetic engineering and behavioural manipulation—the super-industrial peoples will be able to break out of further limits to material growth. According to this scenario the most important new breakthroughs

25

will continue to be geographical and physical, economic and technical. The assumption is that if European, scientific, expansionist, economic, masculine man will have the courage of his convictions, he will be able to brush aside (or at least bring under control) the political, social and psychological problems, as well as the economic problems, that beset industrialised societies today.

This approach to the future implies an ethic of élitism and domination in a class-divided world. Internationally it implies that, by becoming super-industrialised as the less developed countries become industrialised, today's industrialised countries will maintain their economic superiority. It implies that within each super-industrialised country there will be two sharply polarised classes—a responsible technocratic élite in charge of every important sphere of life, and the irresponsible unemployed masses with little to do but enjoy their leisure. Apart from one's moral reservations about this scenario, there are strong doubts about its technical and economic feasibility, and it also seems quite unrealistic from a political, social and psychological point of view. It may be best to regard it as a Utopian projection of the fantasies of the dominant technocratic élites in the affluent countries today.

A SANE, HUMANE, ECOLOGICAL (SHE) FUTURE

This contrasting view of post-industrial society is based on the assumption that the most important new frontiers are now psychological and social (personal and human); not technical and economic. Whereas the industrial revolution was primarily about the development of things, the post-industrial revolution will be primarily about the development of people; it will enable human beings to break out of the psychological and social limits that thwart further progress today, just as the industrial revolution enabled them to break out of the constraints that limited their technical and physical capabilities 200 years ago. This means that the transition from industrial to post-industrial society will involve a change of direction, not an acceleration of industrial trends.

Among the foreseeable changes of direction will be the following:

- from economic growth to human growth;
- from polarisation of sex roles in society to a new balance between them;
- from increasing specialisation to increasing self-sufficiency;
- from increasing dependence on big organisations and professional know-how to increasing self-reliance;
- from increasing urbanisation to a more dispersed pattern of

26

habitation;
- from increasing centralisation to more decentralisation of power;
- from increasing dependence on polluting technologies that waste resources and dominate the people who work with them to increasing emphasis on technologies appropriate to the environment, to the availability of resources, and to the needs of people; and
- from increasing emphasis on rationality and the left-hand side of the brain to increasing emphasis on intuition and the right-hand side of the brain.

In this paper I am dealing with the post-industrial revolution only as it will affect the 'overdeveloped' countries. However, it should be noted that these changes of direction will apply also to 'less developed' countries, where a needs-oriented approach to development may already be superseding the pursuit of blind economic growth. So far as the international economic order is concerned, SHE post-industrialists (by contrast with their HE opponents) aim for economic convergence between overdeveloped and underdeveloped countries, which will enable all the inhabitants of the planet to achieve an adequate and sustainable level of material life early in the next century. This approach is sometimes called 'Another Development'.[4]

We can imagine what this change of direction will involve by remembering that industrialisation has tended to shift activities (growing food, baking bread, caring for old people, for example) out of the informal part of the economy in which work is done for love into the formal part in which work is done for money. In the HE future this tendency would be accentuated; many activities still carried on today in informal, interpersonal, familial, neighbourly relationships would become the formalised work of paid professionals attending to the needs of customers and clients. In the SHE future, on the other hand, this tendency will be reversed. People will live a greater part of their lives in and around their homes and local communities, doing more for themselves and for one another. People will become more self-reliant, more familial, more neighbourly. Work, leisure, education, and family life will become more closely integrated, not more fragmented. The different compartments—schooling, work, retirement—in which the young, the adult and the elderly are now expected to live their lives, will begin to break down.

This change of direction will involve reversing today's increasing financial indebtedness (through mortgages, hire purchase, credit cards, etc.) and increasing financial commitments (to pensions, insurance policies, etc.) that now keep people's noses to the grindstone of paid work. It will require

---

[4] See, for example, *What Now? Another Development*, Dag Hammarskjold Foundation, Uppsala, Sweden, 1975.

new financial institutions—local enterprise trusts, appropriate technology investment bonds, ecological land bonds, land trusts, etc.—that will enable people to invest their spare money in developments that they themselves support. It will involve many other reforms of the existing monetary and financial system (national and international), allowing people and localities to take more control over their personal and local interests, and to reduce their dependence on outside sources of money.

In the SHE future an education system mainly geared to the acquisition of paper qualifications will become increasingly irrelevant. Education will aim at preparing young people for a job (if they have one), and for useful and rewarding unemployment (if they do not), and (in either case) for personal growth and a good quality of adult life. Education will be recognised as an aspect of life that should continue from the cradle to the grave, and not as something provided during childhood and adolescence by professional teachers in special institutions called schools and colleges. As the prevailing concept of education develops in this way, increasing numbers of young people will wish to become more deeply involved in real-life activities centred around their homes and local communities. At the same time, changing patterns of work, leisure and retirement will be involving adults and elderly people more deeply in these activities, too. These changes will soften existing demarcation lines, not only between men and women and between old and young, but also between education, work, leisure, preparing and growing food, and many other aspects of personal and community life.

In short, as we move into the SHE future, more and more people will perceive the need to liberate themselves and one another from excessive dependence on the system—for their employment, social services, health, education, politics, and so on. At the same time, more and more people working in the system will begin to perceive the need to 'decolonise' it before it breaks down; that is, to enable people to reduce their dependence on it and become more self-reliant. These concepts of liberation and decolonisation are central to my theme.

THE NATURE OF THE CHALLENGE

A post-industrial revolution on these lines, involving a change of direction from material growth to personal and social growth, will be as large a historical change as the Industrial Revolution two hundred years ago. How will a change of this magnitude come about? And what can we do to help it come about as smoothly and peacefully as possible?

First, we can learn useful lessons from the Industrial Revolution itself.

The Industrial Revolution was not brought about by enlightened government policies. It was not brought about by political revolution. It happened because an old way of life had reached its limits, because innovators and entrepreneurs then opened up new space, and because multitudes of people then followed them into it in a self-sustaining cumulative process. The innovations and new enterprises of that time were of a technical and economic nature. They have altered the whole character of society—the ways people work and live and think. The innovations and new enterprises of the post-industrial revolution will be personal and human, social and psychological. They, too, will alter the whole character of society. Social and psychological innovators and social and psychological entrepreneurs will provide the shock troops for the post-industrial revolution.

Second, we should understand that the industrialised way of life is breaking down, and we need a breakthrough to a post-industrial way of life. This immediately suggests three vital tasks: to speed up the breakthrough; to ease the breakdown; and to help both to come about in such a way that they combine in a single process of evolutionary transformation.

We can speed up the breakthrough by helping to liberate ourselves from too much dependence: on employers for our work; on business corporations for our food and the other goods we need; on the medical profession and the drug companies for our health; on the educational profession and educational institutions for our learning; and on professional priests and religious organisations for our spiritual needs. A very wide range of activity is opening up here in alternative economics, alternative technology, alternative health, alternative education, alternative politics, alternative religion, and many other fields.

We can ease the breakdown by helping other people to become more self-reliant and less dependent. Doctors can help people to become more self-reliant about their health. Engineers can develop small-scale technologies which will enable people to provide for their own energy needs, or to repair their own houses and cars and household equipment, in a more self-reliant way. Government officials can work out policies which will enable people to do more for themselves and one another in their own localities, and thus to become less dependent on government services. These are three examples—doctors, engineers, government officials—of people with professional or managerial positions in 'the system', who can help to ease its breakdown by helping people to become less dependent on them. They will be giving away their own power over these people, before it breaks down. They will be decolonising the system, just as the European powers found it necessary to decolonise their empires.

We can help breakdown and breakthrough to combine in a single process of evolutionary transformation by helping people to understand what is going on, and by helping them to see the future in new ways. For example, we may be able to help protagonists of human scale technologies, organic agriculture, rural resettlement, a small business (or common ownership) economy, alternative approaches to education or health, and so on, to see that these are connected parts of the same new frontier. Or we may be able to help to replace today's industrial concepts of wealth, work, growth, power, and so on with post-industrial concepts as the dominant concepts in people's thinking.

Third, we need to understand the psychological aspects of the post-industrial revolution. It will involve grieving for the industrial age which is passing. It will be like a crisis of adolescence, in which children liberate themselves from their parents, and parents decolonise the relationship with their children. It will be like a mid-life crisis, in which a person rethinks the direction of his life. It will be like a personal breakdown in which the individual's old way of life becomes blocked or collapses around him, until he finds the ultimate reserve of energy which enables him to break through to a new way of life.

A MULTITUDE OF ROLES

The post-industrial revolution will be a pluralist, polymorphous, polycentric process. It will be brought about by many different types of people, acting in many different fields, and interacting with one another in many different roles.

In *The Sane Alternative* I identified ten positive roles, which I called 'transformation roles', as follows:

- people whose aim and skill is to speed the breakdown of the old system by helping to make it inoperable and destroying its credibility; theirs is a *demolition* role;
- people who are trying to improve the old system, by introducing changes that will make it better and stronger; their aim is to avert the breakdown of the old, but their actions may help to ease the transition to the new; theirs is a *reforming* role;
- people who are creating and developing the growth points for a new society; theirs is a *construction* role;
- people who aim to liberate themselves and other people from their present dependence on the existing system of society; theirs is a *liberating* role;

- people who are working to ensure that the old system breaks down as painlessly as possible for everyone who is dependent on it; in managing its collapse, theirs is a *decolonising* role;
- people who, as liberators or as decolonisers, are helping other people to take more control over their own lives—in health, or politics, or learning, or religion, or their economic activities or in any other important aspect of their life; theirs is an *enabling* role;
- people who are changing their personal way of life, and helping other people to change theirs, so that their lives will be more consistent with their image of a sane, humane, ecological future; theirs is a *lifestyle* role;
- people who are exploring and communicating new concepts of power, wealth, work, growth, learning, healing, and so on, appropriate to a sane, humane, ecological society; as the paradigm shifters, the ideological revolutionaries, theirs is a *metaphysical reconstruction* role;
- people who recognise that all these different sorts of people will contribute positively to the transformation of society, and who are working to make sure that the transformation, though polycentric, is a widely understood, widely shared process of conscious evolutionary change; theirs is a *strategic* role;

I also identified four negative or neutral roles:

- people who refuse to countenance the breakdown of the old system and its replacement by a new one; in trying to suppress the activities of the people listed above, theirs is a *reactionary* role;
- people who, having themselves failed in their own attempts to change society in one way or another, are confident that no one else will succeed, and anxious that they should not; they include Nestorian wiseacres, but mainly theirs is the *pessimistic and cynical* role;
- people who are humble (or superior) observers of what is happening and who, while they enjoy talking about it, writing about it, and scoring points off one another about it, do not want to take part; they can be helpful or unhelpful; theirs is the *academic* role;
- and, finally, people who, wanting simply to get on with their own lives in whatever circumstances happen to exist, are not particularly concerned to encourage change or to resist it; theirs is the *routine practitioner* role.

How will people playing these different roles, in many different fields of activity, interact with one another as the post-industrial revolution gathers pace? We cannot discuss this in detail here. But, as in his day Karl Marx confidently expected a general polarisation around the bourgeoisie and the proletariat, so today we should expect all sections of society to polarise to a greater or lesser extent around the two sides of the coming conflict between the protagonists of the HE and SHE visions of post-industrial society.

WHAT WOULD MARX SAY?

A friendly critic recently told me that my thinking seemed to miss the kind of issues which have been the central concerns of the traditional Left. It appeared to be based in:

> what might be termed a liberal conception of the human being and social relations: the individual is a fairly powerful entity, possessing a fair amount of freedom, who can exert influence in the realm of ideas. This is quite plausible from a middle-class vantage-point, but it makes very little sense from that of about 50% of the population of a nation such as Britain. The Left, therefore, has generally dubbed such conceptions as 'bourgeois idealism'—meaning, in effect, a projection from the bourgeois' own place in society. Instead, it has advised us to take very seriously the huge differences in power and in material interests between the classes in society; and it looks for radical social change, not through the work of individuals in 'transformation roles', but through the concerted action of a whole class. Even though such action may bring about some hurt, the argument is that it is the only way that the 'class conflict' can be won.[5]

I understand why I have given this impression. The principal concerns and strategies of the contemporary Left in the industrialised countries carry little more conviction with me than those of the contemporary Right. Nonetheless, as I said at the start of this paper, one of the features of industrialised society today is a widespread sense of personal helplessness, and one of the greatest needs is for a new sense of constructive solidarity that will enable people to act. In this respect, among others, my perception of the situation is similar to Marx's perception of the situation which prevailed in the nineteenth century. Indeed, I suspect that if Marx were living now the prospect of transforming today's industrialised society into the SHE future would grip his imagination, just as strongly, as the prospect of transforming 19th century capitalism into his vision of communism gripped it during his actual lifetime. Marx's thinking bears more directly on the post-industrial revolution than does the thinking of many of his followers living today.[6]

Marx saw that the prevailing economic and social relations between

[5] Personal correspondence from Dr Tom Kitwood, School of Science and Society, University of Bradford, England.

[6] The literature is of course, immense. A useful summary is in A. S. Cohen, *Theories of Revolution*, Nelson, London, 1975.

people in a society corresponded to the stage of economic development which that society had reached. As he said:

> The sum total of these relations of production constitutes the economic structure of society, on which rises a legal and political superstructure, and to which correspond definite forms of social consciousness.

He saw that every society contained inherent—and, as we would now say, escalating—contradictions in its existing structure of relations that would eventually lead to its collapse. This applied to ancient and to feudal society and it applied—so he thought—especially to capitalist or bourgeois society. The future would thus contain a qualitative break. A new kind of society would come into existence. A new epoch would be born.

For such a transformation (or revolution) to occur, Marx pointed out that not only must the objective circumstances have developed to the right point, but the subjective condition must also have arisen. By this he meant that there must be widespread consciousness of the nature of the situation and of the action needed to transform it. He identified alienation as an important ingredient in this widespread growth of consciousness—alienation being the process which leads people to realise they are treated as mere commodities in the kind of society that currently exists. He saw that those who are thus alienated from the dominant values of their society will eventually form a large section of it, drawn together by consciousness of their common condition.

Thus, Marx argued, as the contradictions in the existing structure of economic and social relations become more acute, the most powerful forces in society will polarise around two conflicting sets of interests. The dominant set of interests will be enforced by the dominant section of society. The opposing set of interests will be developed by the alienated section of society, which the dominant section has brought into existence in opposition to it. Because of the contradictions in the existing structure of society, either the alienated section will eventually win its struggle for liberation, or the whole society will collapse.

In all this, Marx's thinking helps our understanding of what the post-industrial revolution will involve and what will bring it about. There are, however, two crucial differences in the situation as it exists today and as it existed in the nineteenth century. The first concerns the two sides in the struggle. The second concerns the role of the State.

In industrial societies today, the structure of relations between people who own the means of production and people who sell their labour has changed so fundamentally since Marx that it no longer throws up two separate classes of people. Every inhabitant of Britain, for example, is now an owner of the means of production, through insurance companies, pension funds, or public corporations (including nationalised industries); at the same time, the majority of active people are now paid employees. The bourgeoisie and the proletariat, in Marx's sense, no longer exist. Their heirs today are the people who are trying to create a technocratic (HE) future and those who, emerging in opposition to them, are trying to create a humane (SHE) future. These are the opponents whose conflict is beginning to provide the motor force for the post-industrial revolution.

In Marx's day it was reasonable to argue that the main function of the State was to provide the ruling class with an instrument of control and, in the last resort, of violence with which to dominate the rest of society. According to Marx, therefore, the revolutionary class must take over the State, turn it into their own instrument for dominance and control, and use it to effect the revolutionary transformation of the old form of society into the new. That transformation would consist of rooting out the remains of the previous ruling class, eliminating the class antagonisms surviving from their period of dominance, and enabling a new society—a new set of social and economic relationships—to emerge 'in which the free development of each is the condition for the free development of all'. The emergence of that new society would permit, and at the same time require, the State to wither away, since a ruling class would no longer exist which might need to impose its will upon society by force. The State could thus be expected to decolonise itself (in my terminology), to give away its powers over people, and to enable people to exercise power for themselves.

Marxists still approach the transformation of society as a two-stage process on these lines, with the State playing a centrally important role. They have been mainly concerned with questions arising at the first stage, when the revolutionary class takes over the State and establishes its own rule. Such questions have revolved around the identity of the revolutionary class (e.g. are peasants included as well as workers?) and about the role of the revolutionary party (e.g. should it lead the masses and impose revolutionary goals upon them from outside, or should it merely enable them to channel their energies into the achievement of revolutionary goals which are their own?). In general, Marxist thinkers have devoted much less attention to the question of how the second stage is to be accomplished—how, once established, the dictatorship of the revolutionary class will decolonise itself, dismantle the State, and bring the new society into existence. The great exception is Mao, of course. Having led the revolutionary Chinese masses successfully through the first stage, he developed the strategy of permanent revolution to ensure that, even if the second stage were not accomplished, at least it would not be altogether forgotten.

As post-Marxists we may agree with the classical Marxist view that the State reflects and aims to perpetuate the prevailing structure of economic and social relations. Like all institutions the State is, in cybernetic terms, 'programmed to produce itself'.[7] It is 'dynamically conservative'.[8] Its transformation—in a sense, its withering away—will be an important feature of the post-industrial revolution. Where the post-Marxist goes beyond the traditional Marxist is in recognising that the complex of institutions that make up the late twentieth-century industrialised State is qualitatively different from the nineteenth-century European State experienced by Hegel and Marx, and the twentieth century Russian and Chinese States experienced by Lenin and Mao. This means that the classical Marxist two-stage strategy of revolutionary transformation—first take over the State and then use the State as an instrument with which to dismantle itself—is no longer valid, if indeed it ever was.

Two developments, in particular, have changed the nature of the State. In the first place, the kind of corporate Welfare State that has now grown up in a country like Britain extends its activities right through industry, the trade unions, social services, professions and other parts of society. As I have said, the people who carry out its functions no longer represent a different class of people from the rest. In their different roles as pupils, students, workers, customers, taxpayers, patients, savers, pensioners, etc., most people belong on both sides of the old divide between society and the State. In this sense the people have already infiltrated the State and taken it over. By contrast with an earlier stage of industrial capitalism, when people of one class may have used the State to dominate and exploit people of another, one of the main features of today's industrial societies is that people use the extended State to dominate and exploit one another, and even to dominate and exploit themselves, wearing another hat. In the second place, the process which I have referred to elsewhere as 'dismantling the Nation State' is gathering momentum. In Britain, for example, the increase of international government activity and power at European and world levels, together with increasing pressure for the devolution of power to Scotland and Wales and other 'regions', and also to the truly local level, has begun to whittle away the significance of national sovereignty. Both these developments have outdated the idea of a revolutionary takeover of the State. It has become both pointless and unfeasible.

This explains why traditional left-wing approaches to the future of industrial society now lack credibility. The following comments on three

[7] Stafford Beer, *Designing Freedom*, John Wiley, 1974.
[8] Donald Schon, *Beyond The Stable State*, Penguin, 1973.

recent British approaches of this kind are relevant:

> Stuart Holland's proposals for a programme of full, centrally-controlled,
> nationalisation seem to depend excessively on the rationality and public-
> spiritedness of governments and trade unions, for which there is little historical
> evidence. Moreover, in the face of his own evidence he nowhere shows how
> national governments can control the operations of the multinational
> companies, which evidently are in a position to adapt their strategies to suit the
> circumstances of any particular nation state. Glyn and Sutcliffe look forward to
> 'the control by the working class of its own fate in a democratic socialist system',
> but they don't anywhere spell out how this is going to be achieved, and certainly
> give no evidence that the working class movement itself is moving in this
> direction in Britain...Nairn's vision is frankly apocalyptic. The British political
> system will fragment, and out of the ashes of a disintegrated United Kingdom
> will rise the phoenix of the English working class, the bourgeois scales finally
> fallen from its eyes, and capable at last of realising its common struggle and
> common destiny with the international working class movement.[9]

As awareness spreads that traditional Marxist strategies now lack
credibility in the industrialised West, and that the situation has developed
beyond the capacity of traditional Marxist theory to explain and transform, a
new consciousness is emerging in opposition to the dominant values and the
dominant system of today's society. It is a consciousness of being exploited,
deprived, de-humanised, and alienated, just as Marx described. But we feel
that the exploitation, deprivation, and dehumanisation are now imposed as
much by ourselves as by others. The new consciousness is of people becoming
aware of the need to liberate themselves and one another from dependence on
the system. This consciousness represents what Marx would have called the
subjective condition for the post-industrial revolution. Those in whom it is
rising are beginning to form what Marx would have called the new
'revolutionary class'.

A NON-VIOLENT REVOLUTION

So, reverting to the title of this paper—responsibility and response-ability—
what should we do and what can we do?

I have made it clear that I hope the post-industrial revolution will be a
non-violent transformation of industrialised society. It will happen because
industrialised society is breaking down and because people are beginning to

[9] Krishan Kumar, 'Thoughts on the Present Discontents in Britain', to be published in *Theory
and Society*. The References are to: Stuart Holland, *The Socialist Challenge*, Quartet, 1975; A.
Glynn and B. Sutcliffe, *British Capitalism, Workers, and the Profits Squeeze*, Penguin, 1972; and
Tom Nairn, *The Break-Up of Britain*, New Left Books, 1977.

see a better alternative to it. It will happen because more and more people are beginning to understand that by liberating themselves from excessive dependence on the system which industrialised society has created, they can enjoy a better quality of life, and that by liberating themselves from unnecessary material wants they can develop themselves more richly as people.

In every department of their lives there is a multitude of ways in which people can begin—many have already begun—to liberate themselves, and help one another to do the same. There is no need to try to destroy the system or take it over. It will be enough to withdraw support from it: to work rather less in the paid job, and rather more at unpaid work at home and in the local neighbourhood; to spend rather less money on food, or repairs, or entertainment, and to give rather more time to growing food, doing repairs, and creating entertainment for oneself, one's family and one's neighbours; to give rather less time and attention to remote forms of politics and rather more time and energy to important local issues that affect the life of oneself and one's friends more closely; and so on. As more and more people become aware that more and more people are doing this, more and more people will become conscious of belonging to the new 'revolutionary class'.

It would be naïve to suppose that everyone in dominant positions will be eager to give their power away, or that everyone in dependent positions will be eager to liberate themselves. Domination is what provides a sense of security and self-worth for some people; dependence is what provides it for others. The SHE vision of the post-industrial future will be rejected by both these types. As the SHE prospect becomes more likely, the possibility of mass psychosis among the HE types, leading to new forms of fascism, cannot be ignored. They will do all they can to create the HE future, with its dominant technocratic élite and its dependent, irresponsible masses. Failing that, they will try to impose Totalitarian Clampdown as second best.

But there is also a more favourable side to the situation. As industrialised society reaches its limits and begins to break down, more and more people in managerial and professional positions are beginning to feel they are imprisoned in worthless roles. They find it less easy to help, or to dominate, those who are supposed to be dependent on them. They begin to yearn for a more convivial, more familial, more neighbourly life for themselves. They begin to see that their own liberation depends on giving their power away. They begin to want to help their customers or their clients to be less dependent on them. They begin to think about the changes and reforms that will be necessary in order to decolonise their part of the system. As these people decide to change the direction of their own lives they will, *ipso facto*, be deciding to change the structure of relations in society. It is of such changes in the existing structure of relations that the post-industrial revolution will consist.

CONCLUSION

There are many crucial questions, especially about the organisation necessary to carry out the post-industrial revolution and about its international aspects, which there is no time or space to discuss here and now. But let me conclude by saying briefly why I believe that our two countries—Britain and Canada—may both be expected to play important parts in it.

Britain, as I have said, was the first industrial nation and is among the first to reach the limits of industrialism. We have never committed ourselves as wholeheartedly to material economic success as have some other peoples, such as the Germans, the Americans, and the Japanese. Our recent economic problems have, to some extent, reflected our preference for quality of life.

I believe that, in fact, the post-industrial revolution has already started in Britain. One morning we shall wake up and realise that, in spite of the exhortations of the economic Cassandras, we have been beginning to move unconsciously and crabwise into the post-industrial future.

In Canada, of all the other countries I know, one finds the most healthy scepticism about a Business-As-Usual future based on indefinite economic growth and the continuing sovereignty of the Nation State. I am aware of more serious thinking in Canada at all levels of society about the prospect of a post-industrial society than in any other country. This thinking covers the possibilities and practical implications of a more conserving society, a more familial society, and a more needs-oriented approach to Third World development—including, by an extension of that concept—the future development of the indigenous peoples of Canada.

That is why I expect both Britain and Canada to play important parts in the post-industrial revolution, with citizens of both our countries continuing to work on it together.

7 St Ann's Villas, London
1978

3

The Political Economy
of a Conserving Society

This paper was given at a meeting of PARLIGAES, the Parliamentary Liaison Group on Alternative Energy Strategies, organised by Renée-Marie Croose-Parry, at the House of Commons, London on 4th December 1979. It has not been previously published.

PARLIGAES still exists and is, indeed, going strong but under another name. It is now called the Parliamentary Renewable And Sustainable Energy Group (PRASEG), and is based at the International Institute for Energy Conservation.

Renée-Marie Croose Parry now lives in Florida. At the time of writing this, Alison Pritchard and I are about to go to Cuba for a conference on environment and society which she is helping to organise there.

January 1997

The Political Economy of a
More Conserving Society

Ralph Waldo Emerson, the American essayist and philosopher, once said that 'the English mind turns every abstraction it can receive into a portable utensil or working institution'. That is a suitable text for this paper. My aim is to provide a sketch map of the terrain, so to speak, in which decisions about energy alternatives are being and will be made. So, although the subject sounds rather abstract, I believe that what I have to say has practical relevance for anyone who has to decide on, or who wishes to influence, alternative energy strategies.

The paper has three main sections. The first deals with the shifts that are currently taking place in our perceptions of political economy, and the second with the comparable shift that is taking place in our approach to the use of resources. Against that general background, the third section discusses some specific questions raised by the prospect of reducing the use of energy, whether to support our present way of life or to meet the energy needs of a society whose direction of development has significantly changed.

CHANGING PERCEPTIONS OF POLITICAL ECONOMY[1]

How do political and economic decisions get made? How should they be made? Different people operate with different perceptions—different conceptual models of the processes of politics and the economy, and different assumptions about which issues are fundamental. In this section I shall discuss several different models (all of which are alive, if not well, today) and suggest that the balance is shifting between them—in other words, that what has been called a paradigm shift is taking place in the sphere of political economy.

Three conventional models of political economy have been competing with one another in late industrial Britain. They are models of how political and economic decision-making ought to be structured. We all know what they are. So I shall summarise them baldly, and indicate what kind of

[1] C. B. Macpherson, *The Life and Times of Liberal Democracy* (Oxford University Press, 1977), provides a stimulating analysis of successive models of liberal democracy.

measures for achieving a more efficient use of energy are implied by each.

Model 1 is the market model originally developed by Adam Smith. Identified with it today [i.e. in 1979] are politicians like Sir Keith Joseph and economists like those belonging to the Institute of Economic Affairs.[2] Its assumptions are that people act as individuals bent on maximising their own economic benefit; if they are left free to do so, the price mechanism will automatically bring supply and demand into balance, and the invisible hand of the market place will ensure that the outcome is the greatest possible benefit to the greatest possible number of people. According to this view, it can and should be left to rising energy prices and falling energy supplies to do what is necessary to bring about energy conservation and more efficient energy use.

Model 2, at the other extreme, is the model of the beneficent state. Identified with it today [1979] are politicians on the Labour Left like Tony Benn. The assumption is that governments have the capacity and should have the will to take optimal economic decisions and allocate resources optimally on behalf of the people. Those who take this view favour centralised economic planning by the state, including comprehensive national energy planning, and government control of important economic activities—the 'commanding heights' of the economy. So far as energy conservation is concerned, rationing by regulation is preferred to rationing by price; government R. and D. programmes should develop energy saving techniques and processes, and government policies should diffuse them.

Model 3, between these two extremes, is the model of the mixed economy, corrected market economy, or managerial economy. This is associated with the 'moderate' wings of the Conservative and Labour parties and with the Liberals, and involves a degree of co-operation between the corporate estates of the realm—business, labour and government, in particular. In practice, this has been the dominant model in Britain for most of the last 30 years, the argument having been mainly limited to the desirable mix between market and state, and the required degree of correction of the market by the state. So far as energy is concerned, this model implies—in addition to measures appropriate to the previous two—that taxes and tax concessions, government subsidies and government contracts should be used to encourage more efficient energy use by the private sector.

Two shared assumptions underlie these three models, one economic, the

[2] [1997 footnote. Sir Keith Joseph was outstanding among the leading British Conservatives who, in opposition in the 1970s and after 1979 during the early years of the Thatcher government, helped to develop the 'free market' approach to policy making in many fields. The Institute of Economic Affairs was the 'think tank' most closely associated with this approach.]

other political.

The first is the assumption that objectively optimal economic decisions are available, and that the object of the exercise is to identify these decisions, make them, and implement them. The market model claims that this is all done automatically by the market's invisible hand. The beneficent state and the mixed economy do not have recourse to the invisible hand. They have to rely on magic of a different kind—namely the economic calculations, including cost/benefit calculations, of experts—to discover what the optimal decisions are. In the field of energy policy, for example, a daunting amount of abstruse economic calculation is taking place today.[3]

The second shared assumption concerns the political relationship between the individual and the state. All three models focus on decision-making at the national level in Westminster and Whitehall, coupled with the right of individuals to choose every few years what government they wish to have. Apart from the corporatist tendency of Model 3, none of the three models pays much attention to the plurality of interest groups and organisations, active in both the public and the private sector, which mediate the relationship between the individual and the state. All three models tend to regard the citizen as an individual consumer in the market for political goods.

However, the credibility of this set of models has now worn thin. Whatever the theory may say, market freedom in practice favours the rich and powerful, and fails to bring about adjustments in the use of scarce commodities quickly and smoothly. The theory of the beneficent state is equally naive. In practice, state control is seen to give certain interest groups an unfair share of economic power, and state planning is no more successful than the market in adjusting to the changing availability of resources. The mixed economy appears muddled and inadequate both in theory and in practice. The elaborate economic analyses by which its decisions are theoretically supposed to be validated seem, in their complexity and their ultimate irrelevance to the actual outcome, increasingly like the theological enquiries (how many angels can stand on the point of a pin?) characteristic of medieval society in its declining years.

Another model (Model 4) has therefore been taking the place of the first three in many people's minds. This is a model of conflict. It describes what is, rather than what ought to be. It holds that political and economic decisions are reached by a continuing process of adjustment between competing élites in an oligopolistic market. The three previous models—free market, beneficent state, and mixed economy—are, on this interpretation, merely the labels and banners under which various competing élites group themselves to

---

[3] [This is no less true in 1997 than it was in 1977.]

sell their wares and fight their campaigns.

In my view this model, Model 4, gives a fairly realistic account of how political and economic decisions have been reached in recent years. It applies both to the competition for political power (characterised by success in acquiring votes) in a political market dominated by a small number of big political parties, and to the competition for economic power (characterised by success in acquiring money) in an economic market dominated by giant corporations and big industrial pressure groups. It helps to explain why strategies which seem obviously desirable under Model 3 (the rationally managed mixed economy) attract so little support and such strong opposition. A strategy to encourage traffic to shift from road to rail—and from car to bus—in the interests of safety, amenity, equity and energy conservation, is a case in point.

Model 4 also suggests that decisions about the future of nuclear power will depend less on supposedly objective analyses of economic benefits and costs than on struggles between the political and economic interest groups primarily involved. Not the least important factor here, incidentally, is political fear of the coal-mining industry. Since the Heath government's defeat by the miners in 1974 and the electricity cuts and blackouts of subsequent winters, Conservatives in particular have been afraid of the power of the miners and of the political purposes for which that power might one day be used. This is why it is helpful to the nuclear industry to have a militant miners' leader prominent among their opponents. He reinforces the feeling in many people's minds that a bigger nuclear industry would be a useful countervailing force against the kind of threat which he himself represents.[4]

Model 4, then, leads us to recognise that decisions, including future decisions about energy, will be shaped by sets of interests and considerations much more widely ranging than simple pursuit of economic gain, public interest, or a mixture of the two. It helps us to reject the utilitarian myth that there is one best set of decisions for society and that any argument revolves around what that set of decisions might be. The pluralist model enables us to perceive that every decision favours some people and disadvantages others, and that the argument is about who is to benefit and who is to suffer. In public policy research, including research into energy options, this implies a form of cost/benefit analysis which works out who is likely to get what benefits and who is likely to pay what costs, in place of the conventional form which purports to make an objective calculation of total benefits and total costs. The

---

[4] [1997 footnote. The reference here, obvious in 1979, was to Arthur Scargill. Subsequently, the defeat of the 1984/5 miners' strike by the Thatcher government led not only to the run-down of the coal-mining industry but also to a weakening of Conservative support for nuclear energy.]

same applies to employment impact analysis. We don't want global figures. We want to know what sort of people in what sort of places are likely to gain and to lose what sort of jobs.[5]

But that is not quite the end of this part of the story. Model 4 itself is now being increasingly questioned. The competing political and economic institutions of late industrial society are felt to be overdeveloped. The thrust of industrialism has led to the monetisation of many goods and services that used to be exchanged in family, neighbourly or other interpersonal relations of a social kind, to the professionalisation of knowledge and function previously open to all, and to the centralisation (for example, in London) of political and economic power on which local life is now dependent. A dominant feature of political and economic argument in the coming years is likely to be a sharpening conflict between those who want these trends to continue and those who are working for a change of direction. I have discussed at greater length in *The Sane Alternative* the two contrasting visions of post-industrial society—technocratic and humane—which underlie this conflict.

According to this perception, the competing élites of Model 4 are only one half of the picture, the other half being the people—whether as individuals, or as members of groups, or as residents of localities—whom the élites aim to keep in a state of dependency. While the élites may compete against one another in a 'horizontal' dimension, the more important fact is that they co-operate collectively with one another (as Big Brother) in 'vertical' opposition to the people. Thus whereas Model 4 focuses on conflict between the coal and nuclear industries as two competing élites, the emerging new model of political economy, Model 5, perceives them both as belonging to an overdeveloped, dominant production system, whose interests are in conflict with the best interests of people.

In other words, Model 5 focuses on the conflict between the interests that benefit from centralisation and dependency and the interests that would benefit from decentralisation and self-reliance. As regards energy use and energy supply, it recognises the scope for more self-sufficiency in energy at every level—for households, factories and offices, localities and regions—as

---

[5] David Elliott, in *Energy Options and Employment*, CAITS, 1979, has made a start. [1997 note. CAITS, the Centre for Alternative Industrial and Technological Systems, had been set up by Mike Cooley and his Colleagues from the Lucas Aerospace Combine Shop Stewards' Committee to promote the concepts of socially useful production and human-centred technologies on which their dispute with Lucas Aerospace had been based. 'The choices are essentially political and ideological. As we design technological systems, we are in fact designing sets of social relationships, and as we question those social relationships and attempt to design systems differently, we are then beginning to challenge in a political way, power structures in society—Mike Cooley, *Architect Or Bee?*, 1979.]

an alternative to dependence on large, remote, nationally and internationally controlled sources of supply, whether dominated by coal miners, nuclear engineers, or oil sheikhs. And it recognises that energy conservation makes a direct contribution to greater self-reliance.

As Model 5 begins to replace Model 4 as the basic model of conflict in society, it points towards the emergence of a new decentralised model (Model 6), which will compete with Models 1, 2 and 3 as a normative description of how political and economic decision-making ought to be structured. Many people are already working to clarify this model in industrialised and Third World countries alike. They refer to it under terms like 'alternative society' or 'another development'.

For practical purposes, I believe that these six models—Models 1, 2, 3, and 6 being ideas of how political economy should work, and 4 and 5 being models of conflicts that actually exist—embody the basic political assumptions and perceptions which will bear significantly on the energy debate and on energy decisions in the coming years But a concluding reference to Marxism may be in place. Model 2—the beneficent state—is the closest of the five to conventional Marxism. Model 5, as I have discussed elsewhere,[6] has interesting similarities and dissimilarities with Marxism. Few people today are unaffected by Marx's insights—as by Darwin's and Freud's— but it seems likely that the impact of Marxist thinking on British politics and economics will continue to be mediated through models such as those sketched here, rather than through a specifically Marxist model. So far as energy policy is concerned, for example, it is not readily apparent what a Marxist energy policy for Britain would entail.

A MORE CONSERVING SOCIETY

Hazel Henderson speaks of the progression of Western economies from the 'soaring sixties' through the 'stagflation seventies' to the 'economising eighties'.[7] She calls herself a counter-economist. But you do not have to be a counter-economist to recognise that, as we now enter the 1980s, we are almost certainly entering a period in which the husbanding of resources—including energy—will receive more attention than in the recent past. By 'recent past' some people mean the period of 35 years since World War Two, others the 100-year period of the Petroleum Age, others again the 200-year period of the Fossil Fuel Age (corresponding roughly to the Industrial Age). But however

[6] The Politics and Economics of HE and She, *Built Environment*, Vol. 4, No. 4, 1978.
[7] Hazel Henderson, *Creating Alternative Futures*, Berkley Windhover, New York, 1978.

you define the recent past, you will—if you are a realist—expect our society to be at least somewhat more conserving from now on.

The recent shift in the way we think about resources is significant. The distinction between non-renewable and renewable resources is quite new for most of us. But it is now obvious that it makes sense to treat non-renewable resources as capital to be conserved and invested for future returns, and renewable resources as income to be spent up to but not beyond their replacement rate, i.e. the rate at which they can be renewed. It is less widely perceived as yet—but the idea is hovering on the brink of our awareness— that, in addition to non-renewable and renewable resources, an important third category of resources exists: resources which can be positively developed and increased by using them fully. These latent resources include in particular the energies and skills and capabilities of people.

Until recently, the practical implications of conserving natural resources seemed to get more attention from public policy analysts and business strategists in North America than in Britain or Europe. (A couple of years ago I was involved in work by the Canadian Government on 'Canada as a Conserver Society',[8] and in the preparation of guidance given by SRI International (formerly the Stanford Research Institute) to its international business clients about 'Voluntary Simplicity' and 'Business Success in an Equilibrium Economy'.[9]) On the technical scope for energy conservation, the work of British researchers like Gerald Leach[10] compares more directly with that of their opposite numbers in North America like Robert Socolow.[11] No doubt the reason why political and business thinking on the implications of a more conserving society has been slower to get off the ground in Britain is because in recent years most of our political and business thinkers have been so heavily committed to the issues thrown up by the conflicts of Left v. Right and labour v. management.

Fortunately, this is now beginning to change. And, at the more academic level, the work of modern American economists like Herman Daly[12] on a 'steady state economy' and Kenneth Boulding[13] on 'spaceship economics' has certainly been paralleled by that of modern British economists like E. J. Mishan[14] on the costs of economic growth, Fred Hirsch[15] on the social limits

[8] *Canada as a Conserver Society: Resource Uncertainties and the Need for New Technologies*, Science Council of Canada, Report No. 27, 1977.

[9] James Robertson, *Business Success in an Equilibrium Economy*, SRI International, 1977.

[10] Gerald Leach, *A Low Energy Strategy for the United Kingdom*, International Institute for Enviroment and Development (IIED), 1979

[11] Robert H. Socolow, *The Coming Age of Conservation*, Annual Review of Energy, Vol. 2, 1977.

[12] Herman Daly (ed.), *Toward a Steady State Economy*, Freeman, 1973.

[13] Kenneth Boulding, *The Economics of the Coming Spaceship Earth*, (in Daly above).

to growth, and of course E. F. Schumacher[16] on economics as if people mattered. Going further back, two of the best-known political economists in British history, J. S. Mill in *Principles of Political Economy* in 1857 and J. M. Keynes in *Economic Possibilities for our Grandchildren* in 1930, both looked forward to the time when material growth would come to an end and we could concentrate on quality of life.

Industrial society is a production-oriented society, dominated by producers of goods, commodities and services—industry, commerce, government, and professions—rather than by their users. It is also a masculine society, in which high priority is given to the satisfaction which grown-up boys can get out of designing and making and playing with new technological toys. You need look no further than this year's and last year's programmes of PARLIGAES meetings to see how dominated they are by men, most of whom still want to discuss alternative ways of producing energy rather than alternative ways of using it. As questions about the efficiency with which we use resources and the purposes for which we use them grow in urgency and importance, masculine producer interests which want to preserve or increase their existing power are increasingly likely to see the shift towards a more conserving society as a threat.

Thus two types of conflict in the energy debate will increasingly cut across one another. First, there will be conflict of the conventional type between different producer interests—PWR against AGR reactors, for example—and their political associates, seeking to strengthen their relative positions in the economy. I visualise these as 'horizontal' conflicts in the context of Model 4 discussed above. Second, there will be conflict between the energy producers on the one hand, pressing in general for new developments in energy production, and on the other hand the user/citizen interest demanding that top priority should be given to more efficient and economic energy use. I visualise this as a 'vertical' conflict in the context of Model 5. In general, producer interests will argue that further quantitative growth is desirable and feasible, while citizen interests will press the claims of qualitative growth. Questions about the meaning (or meaninglessness) of statistical measures like GNP will feature increasingly in the debate.

One last point about conservation generally. There is no doubt that the increasing urgency of conserving energy and other natural resources, and using them better, will provide exciting problems for scientists, engineers and architects, exciting commercial opportunities for industrialists and business

[14] E. J. Mishan, *The Costs of Economic Growth*, Penguin, 1969.
[15] Fred Hirsch, *Social Limits To Growth*, Routledge Kegan Paul, 1977.
[16] E. F. Schumacher, *Small is Beautiful*, Blond and Briggs, 1973.

people, and exciting challenges for policy-makers in government and the public services. But in itself the idea of a more conserving society is not very inspiring. It smacks of restraint. It can all too easily seem negative and grudging. The conservation of amenity can be a cover for the conservation of privilege. The conservation of resources can be used by rich people and rich countries as an argument for asking poorer people and poorer countries to tighten their belts. Only when the idea of a more conserving society is seen as one aspect of a larger, more positive vision of the future, is it likely to become an important energising force. I shall return to this point later.

USING LESS ENERGY

Theoretically, energy can be conserved *either* by reducing energy intensity, in other words by increasing the efficiency with which energy is used for particular activities, *or* by reducing the level of the activities themselves, *or* by a combination of both. For example, you can increase the efficiency of your car and the way you drive it, to get the same mileage for less petrol; or you can reduce your mileage; or you can do both. You can increase the efficiency of your home heating, to maintain the same temperature for less expenditure of fuel; or you can reduce the temperature of your home; or you can do both.

I shall start by discussing some of the implications of improving energy efficiency while maintaining a conventional development path, and then move on to the possibility of shifting to an alternative development path which would, among other things, involve greatly reduced consumption of energy.

The Leach Report on a Low Energy Strategy for the United Kingdom[17] concluded that the general level of economic activity in Britain could double or treble by the year 2025, without requiring a higher use of primary energy than today. This conclusion was based on a sector-by-sector analysis of the potential scope for greater energy efficiency in the domestic, industrial, commercial and institutional, and transport sectors and in the energy-producing sector itself.

The Leach Report did not examine in depth the non-technical factors which might encourage or discourage the development and use of energy-conserving innovations in those sectors. In addition to the broad political and economic factors discussed earlier and the obvious financial question whether the savings from a particular innovation are likely to justify the costs, important non-technical factors will include: the perceived objectives of

[17] See footnote 10 above.

managements and their efficiency; the readiness of organised workers to accept change; the scope for changing design conventions and accounting conventions; the scope for changing the professional education of builders, engineers, planners, and so on; and the responsiveness of the internal decision-making processes in firms and other organisations. Many of these factors as constraints on innovation generally were discussed at a conference on Technology Choice held in London last year by the British Association for the Advancement of Science and the Intermediate Technology Development Group.[18] The same factors will obviously affect the introduction of energy conserving innovations.

Other questions concern special interest groups. Some consumer organisations are now getting together with environmental groups in a National Energy Efficiency Forum. The social services may also want to work out specific ways in which they could help their clients to meet their needs for fuel and light and power efficiently. Workers in the building trades clearly have an interest in energy conservation. Their trade unions may want to do more to encourage it.

A further set of questions concerns economic distortions. For example, as a general rule the installation of equipment in households—including energy-conserving or, indeed, energy-producing devices—attracts no capital grants or depreciation allowances as does the construction of new oil rigs and pipelines and other energy-producing facilities by commercial firms. Nor does household investment form part of the public investment programme, as does the construction of new power stations. There is thus a systemic bias in favour of energy production by the public and corporate sectors, and against energy conservation (and energy production) in the domestic sector. How might this be removed? (Energy is, of course, only one area in which this general bias exists in favour of the corporate against the domestic sector of the economy.)

But perhaps the crucial factor is how the energy industries perceive their role. Hitherto, the gas and electricity boards, the oil companies and the coal industry have not perceived it as their prime objective to help people to meet their energy needs economically. They have not taken on responsibility for achieving an efficient match between the specific forms of energy supplied

---

[18] Proceedings, *Technology Choice and the Future of Work*, British Association for the Advancement of Science, 1978. [1997 note. The Intermediate Technology Development Group intended to follow this up with a project on technology choice funded by the Gatsby Charitable Foundation. But this did not happen. Nearly twenty years later the need for public understanding and discussion about how decisions are taken about technological innovation, and how the decision-making processes could be changed to take greater account of social and environmental objectives is greater than ever.]

and the specific tasks for which the energy is used. (Using high-cost electricity for low-grade space-heating is an often quoted example of a wasteful mismatch. Amory Lovins[19] compares it to using a chain-saw to cut butter or a forest fire to fry an egg. The energy industries' prime objective has been to meet demand for their product and to sell it in competition with one another. Tariffs, for example, have favoured customers who use more, not less. The forceful marketing of appliances has encouraged customers to use more, not less. There has been no question of positively encouraging and helping all customers to adopt the optimal mix of gas, oil, electricity, solid fuel and energy conservation for their particular needs.

I am not blaming the energy industries for this, or suggesting that they have altogether ignored the need for energy conservation. That would be unfair and untrue. The question is, how might the energy industries be motivated to regard it as part of their prime function to improve the energy efficiency of their customers? Could the objectives of the nationalised energy industries as formally laid down by statute be revised with this in view?[20] What comparable obligations could be placed on the oil companies? Could new pricing policies, new management objectives and new criteria of management success be worked out for the energy industries which would positively encourage conservation?[21]

Suggestions of this kind call in question the conventional economic assumption that growth, including the growth of production and sales by nationalised industries, is the main criterion of success. Is it reasonable to expect managers in the energy industries to discard that assumption, if no one else does? Although the Leach Report assumed that the energy sector alone would embrace conservation as a prime goal, while conventional growth would remain the goal for other sectors of the economy, it may be more realistic to assume that a serious re-orientation towards conservation in the energy industries will only take place as part of a shift towards a more conserving development path for the economy as a whole. That would, of course, open up even greater scope for energy conservation than

[19] Amory Lovins, *Soft Energy Paths*, Penguin, 1977.

[20] [1997 note. Following denationalisation of the UK energy industries it is no longer possible simply to legislate a change in their objectives. Raising the price of energy by replacing existing taxes with higher taxes on energy, as proposed in Chapters 13 and 16 below, may now be the best way to give an incentive to the energy industries to see themselves as providers of services rather than suppliers of commodities.]

[21] *The Changing Expectations of Society in the Next Thirty Years*, the report of a recent international conference on the future of Management Development held by the American Assembly of Collegiate Schools of Business and the European Foundation for Management Development, identified the management of conservation as an increasingly important area of opportunity and challenge for management generally.

Leach envisaged.

There are, in fact, many ways in which the search for energy efficiency necessarily brings wider patterns of activity under review. When we consider systematically the specific uses for which energy is needed in specific places—whether in a house, a factory, a district, a city, or a region—and the total system of energy provision and conservation that would meet those needs most efficiently in each particular case, we find that conventional building practices, conventional planning regulations, conventional principles for operating the electricity grid, and a wide variety of other conventional ways of doing things are called into question. Any widespread use of combined heat and power, providing power for the grid and heat either for factory use or for district heating, would raise these issues.

Finally, as the efficient use of energy takes on a higher priority during the coming years, there can be little doubt that, as in other spheres, diseconomies of scale will become more and more apparent. A 'decentralised, total systems' approach will increasingly often be seen as the best way to enable users to meet their needs efficiently. One consequence may be that decisions about how the energy needs of districts, cities and regions are to be met will increasingly be determined by the contribution the various options would make to the total economic well-being of the districts, cities and regions concerned. Once that is accepted, we are already on a very different development path from that of the last thirty years.

The possibility is, in fact, becoming increasingly clear that countries like Britain may soon change direction to a new development path. There are at least three reasons for this. First, limits—both the physical limits evidenced by resource shortages and environmental pollution, and the social, economic and political limits evidenced by low growth, rising unemployment, inflation, and social stress—may compel us to do so. Second, increasing numbers of people may opt for quality of life rather than further increases in material consumption. Third, for the richer countries to switch to a more conserving path of development may be their most effective way of enabling the poorer countries to develop themselves.

The practicalities of an alternative development path are now being explored in an increasing number of reports and publications. Two which came out this year have the same title, 'Another Britain'. One of these is a Bow Group pamphlet by Nigel Forman, MP.[22] The other is my report to the International Foundation for Development Alternatives (IFDA).[23]

[22] Nigel Forman, *Another Britain*, Bow Group, London, 1979.

[23] James Robertson, *Another Britain*, IFDA, 2 Place du Marché, CH–1260 Nyon, Switzerland, 1979.

Many of us who are in favour of a switch to an alternative development path see it broadly on the following lines:

- **Paid and Unpaid Work.** In manufacturing and services alike there will be further automation of large enterprises supplying mass-produced products and impersonal services. Many people will move into more personal work than they do at present—on small farms, in small firms, in small community enterprises, and in the provision of goods and services on a person-to-person basis. There will be more people working in their own homes and neighbourhoods than there are today; more part-time work; and a fairer distribution of paid and unpaid work between men and women.

- **Industry.** There will be a continuing shift of emphasis towards the recovery and recycling of all kinds of materials, and methods of economising in their use; a shift towards more durable goods, and therefore away from production towards servicing, maintenance and repair; and a shift towards the manufacture of small-scale technologies and equipments for small enterprises and do-it-yourself activities.

- **Food Production and Consumption.** Changes in agriculture and diet will make countries like Britain more self-sufficient in indigenous types of food and less dependent on imported feeding stuffs, butter, etc. There will be less meat in the diet, more smaller farms, part-time farms, and do-it-yourself food-growing.

- **Patterns of Settlement and Patterns of Living.** There will be a more dispersed pattern of settlement countrywide; more people living nearer to their work; more people growing food in cities, more people manufacturing in the country, and more people providing services directly to other people in both; more people spending more active time in and around their own home and locality; more people with their own foodplots and workshops; increasing investment by households and neighbourhoods in all kinds of equipment, including mechanical and telecommunications equipment; more living and working together by children, young people, adults, and the elderly.

- **Decentralisation and Greater Self-Sufficiency.** In general, there will be a shift away from centralisation towards greater autonomy and self-sufficiency at local and regional levels. In particular, localities and regions will strive to become less dependent on external sources of food and energy, recognising that such dependence drains the local 'balance of payments' and that local production for local consumption creates local jobs and a healthy local economy.

The patterns of work, living, transport, production, utilisation of buildings, and decision-making implied by the changes outlined above would be likely to reduce the demand on national energy supply. The energy implications of 'another Britain' clearly merit further attention.

CONCLUSIONS

Let me try to pull together a few threads.

First, some specific points about energy use and conservation arise. PARLIGAES might encourage action on them:

- An analysis is needed of who would stand to gain and who would stand to lose by the introduction of energy conserving measures as envisaged, for example, in the Leach Report.
- Studies are needed of how impediments to such measures could be removed or bypassed, and how potential support for them could be tapped.
- In particular, new management objectives for the energy industries, together with new policies, procedures and performance criteria, need to be worked out that will positively promote energy conservation.
- The possibility of setting up local energy corporations should be examined on the lines of local development corporations or local enterprise trusts. Their purpose would be to help localities, organisations and households to define and meet their energy needs efficiently, and to match the end uses of energy in the locality with potentially available sources of supply. Somewhere like Cornwall, wholly dependent now on energy brought in from outside, might be suitable as a pilot area.[24]
- Energy Research and Development (R&D) programmes should pay special attention, not just to renewable energy sources, but to the development of energy technologies whose social and economic effect is to enable households and localities to be more self-reliant (less

[24] [1997 note. A Cornwall Energy Action plan, prepared by the Cornwall Energy Project (team leader Charmian Larke) was, in fact, published in 1989 by Cornwall County Council, aimed at enabling Cornwall both to reduce its energy needs and to supply a significant proportion of them from local energy production. It was expected to lead to a reduction in the environmental impact of energy systems and provide new business and employment opportunities within the County.]

wholly dependent on Big Brother) in meeting their energy needs.

Second, more generally, more attention needs to be given to future levels and patterns of energy use as they may be affected by changes in energy-using activities. Alternative futures for work; for leisure; for industry, services and agriculture; for travel; for family and neighbourhood living; for the countryside; for the inner city—these are just some of the aspects of the future that will help to determine the demand for energy and the scope for conservation. It is difficult to consider alternative energy strategies seriously, without examining alternative possible futures in these other areas too. Without attempting to become a Parliamentary Liaison Group on Alternative Futures, PARLIGAES may soon have to consider widening its perspective.

Third, I personally see the growing emphasis on energy conservation as part of a wider, general shift of emphasis from production to conservation and efficient use of resources. Moreover, I believe this is beginning to combine with the emergence of a new decentralised model of political economy (Model 6) to create a vision of a post-industrial society in which people are seen to be the most important resource—a society in which more and more people will come to feel that their self-development as members of society is the central project in their lives. In other words, I see a more conserving use of natural resources, including energy, as one aspect of a people-centred post-industrial revolution, which will be comparable in its historical impact to the Industrial Revolution of 200 years ago.

Finally, however, I recognise that although that perception is shared by increasing numbers of people, it is not shared by many others. I recognise that many people, including people involved in energy decisions, still give higher priority to increasing production than to more efficient use. I recognise that many people still operate on political economy Models 1, 2, 3, or 4. I recognise that many people are quite unconcerned about topics such as political economy and a more conserving society; as routine practitioners in a business-as-usual context, they will continue to make their decisions *ad hoc* as circumstances arise. I believe we shall have to keep a sense of all these different perspectives, if we want to understand how decisions about energy are likely to be reached in the coming years, and if we want to contribute effectively to those decisions ourselves.

7 St Ann's Villas, London
1979

4

Work

This chapter is the text of the Voltaire Lecture, given with the title 'The Right To Responsibility In Work' on 1st November 1980, at a conference at High Leigh, Hoddesdon, England on 'Human Rights And Responsibilities'.

The conference was arranged jointly by the Progressive League and the British Humanist Organisation. Owing to my friendship with Peter Cadogan, then Secretary of the humanist congregation called the South Place Ethical Society, I had met a number of humanists—some very progressive, others less so! Margaret Chisman was one of the former. It was she who arranged for me to give this lecture. She is now a director of the Institute for Social Inventions.

The Voltaire Lecture was given annually or biennially for the education of the public about humanism or related aspects of scientific or philosophical thought.

January 1997

Work: The Right to be Responsible

As I see it, my task this evening is threefold. I ought to say something about Voltaire's relevance for us today, since this is the Voltaire lecture. I ought to say something about rights and responsibilities, since this is the subject of your conference. And I ought to say something about work, since this is my chosen topic. I ought, also, of course, to try to weave what I have to say on those three subjects into some kind of unity, and to convey some kind of message or conclusion.

VOLTAIRE'S RELEVANCE TODAY

Voltaire played an important part in one of those transformative periods of history when an old order is breaking down and a new order is breaking through. He lived to see the American Revolution in 1776. He died eleven years before the French Revolution in 1789. He had helped to destroy the credibility of the old form of society dominated by the nobility and the church. He had helped to usher in a new age of science and representative democracy, of industrialism and the nation state.

We today are living in an equally transformative period. After 200 years, the age of industrialism and the nation state is coming towards an end. We are moving into a post-industrial age in which our focus will be global and local, as much as national; in which our concept of the state and the mechanisms of democracy will therefore be transformed; and in which the methods, objectives and results of supposedly objective, rational, scientific enquiry will increasingly be called in question. As the old order continues to break down, we have to prepare the ground for the new order that will take its place. We find, as Voltaire would have found had he been living now, that changes in the dominant concept of work, changes in the way work is organised and distributed, and changes in the rights and responsibilities we attach to work, will be an important feature of the transition.

Voltaire was first and foremost a demolition artist. As Thomas Paine said in *The Rights of Man* (1791), Voltaire's:

> forte lay in exposing and ridiculing the superstitions which priestcraft, united

59

with statecraft, had interwoven with governments. It was not from the purity of his principles or his love of mankind (for satire and philanthropy are not naturally concordant), but from his strong capacity of seeing folly in its true shape, and his irresistible propensity to expose it, that he made these attacks. They were, however, as formidable as if the motives had been virtuous, and he merits the thanks rather than the esteem of mankind.

Paine was a little too dismissive of what he regarded as Voltaire's frivolity and, as I shall later suggest, we should not underestimate Voltaire's constructive contribution to the new thinking of the 18th century Enlightenment in France. But there can be no doubt that Voltaire's first delight, if he had been living today, would have been in satirising many of our modern superstitions.

In place of the superstitions which priestcraft, united with statecraft, had interwoven with governments, Voltaire today would have exposed and ridiculed the superstitions of economistcraft united with statecraft. He would have scorned the notion that by calculating all the costs and benefits involved in some large project, like building a new airport for London, economists, armed with the mysterious knowledge of their craft and with magical aids called computers, could work out what course of action would be best from everyone's point of view. He would have regarded it as a matter of common sense to realise that every course of action will benefit some people and harm others, and that the important question is who is to get the benefit and who is to be harmed. He would have seen that to claim otherwise is to mystify, in the hope of persuading those who are to be harmed to accept it as all for the best.[1]

Voltaire would also have had rare fun with some of the controversies that modern economists get involved in—for example, about the correct way to measure that metaphysical entity called the money supply, or about the relationship between inflation and unemployment. He would have found them extraordinarily reminiscent of the theological controversies which mystified people and darkened their lives in earlier times—for example, about how to measure the space occupied by angels, or about the relationship between the two natures, divine and human, of Jesus Christ.

Voltaire would surely have ridiculed our concern for the Gross National Product, a man-made idol of which we have been persuaded that its size— that only economists know how to measure—is directly proportionate to the happiness of the people of the country over which it presides; an idol, therefore, which has to be fed—in ways which only economists know how to specify—in order to make it as gross as possible. We get an inkling of what Voltaire might have made of the fetish of economic growth from the

---

[1] [1997 note. Chapter 3 touched on this in regard to cost/benefit analysis applied to energy policy.]

following passage by Hugh Stretton.[2] It reminds us that the significance of GNP is closely related to the superstitious reverence given by economists to paid, as contrasted with unpaid, work:

> How easily we could turn the tables on the economists if we all decided that from tomorrow morning, the work of the domestic economy should be paid for. Instead of cooking dinner for her own lot, each housewife would feed her neighbours at regular restaurant rates; then they'd cook for her family and get their money back. We'd do each other's housework and gardening at award rates. Big money would change hands when we fixed each other's tap washers and electric plugs at the plumbers' and electricians' rates. Without a scrap of extra work Gross National Product (GNP) would go up by a third overnight. We would increase that to half if the children rented each other's back yards and paid each other as play supervisors, and we could double it if we all went to bed next door at regular massage parlour rates. Our economists would immediately be eager to find out what line of investment was showing such fabulous growth in capital/output ratio. They'd find that housing was bettered only by double beds and they'd recommend a massive switch of investment into both. Don't laugh, because in reverse, this nonsense measures exactly the distortion we get in our national accounts now.

Now Voltaire did not underestimate the significance of work. At the very end of Candide (1759), for example, he puts the following statements into the mouths of his characters:

> Work wards off three great evils: boredom, vice and poverty. When man was put into the garden of Eden, he was put there that he might till it, that he might work: which proves that man was not born to be idle. Let us work, then, and not argue. It is the only way to make life bearable.

We may feel that these sentiments show a somewhat negative appreciation of the value of work, but at least we may conclude from them, and from what we know of Voltaire's own life, that he regarded working as a centrally important part of living. For that reason, if for no other, he would certainly have brought his scorn and ridicule to bear on some of our other modern superstitions about work. Imagine, for example, how scathing Voltaire would have been about the stupidity, as well as the cruelty, of any government that propagated the harsh morality that all self-respecting citizens should find a job for themselves and, at the same time, took measures that made certain that some millions of citizens would be unable to find one. More fundamentally, Voltaire would surely have ridiculed the idea that full employment is a hallmark of the good society. He would have exposed the shallowness of the assumption that as many people as possible should be dependent on employers to provide

---

[2] [1997 note. I quoted this in Chapter 1, but I think it bears repetition.]

their life's work. What, Voltaire would surely ask, is so good about everyone becoming a wage-slave? I believe he would have seen the progressive society as one which encourages and enables a growing number of its citizens to take the right and the responsibility of defining and organising their own work for themselves, whether as individuals or in association with their fellows.

I said 'progressive' society, and Voltaire believed in progress. It has been said that an optimist is someone who, like Dr Pangloss in *Candide*, believes that we live in the best of all possible worlds, and that a pessimist is someone who fears that we do. On this definition, Voltaire was neither an optimist nor a pessimist. He did not believe that the present state of affairs was good enough, but he did believe that it could be improved. It is a view which most of us probably share.

As progressives, I believe we need to be conscious of three things. First, there are people who don't believe in progress. They are happy with the way things are; they believe in business-as-usual. Or they think things are bound to get worse; they believe in disaster. Some think that history is cyclical; they believe that things go round in circles and that there is very little any of us can do about it. We may disagree with them, but all these kinds of people are part of the situation in which progress is to be made. For practical purposes we should pay some attention to them, because they will have some effect on whether progress happens, what it turns out to be, and how it comes about. This applies to progress towards new ways of conceiving, distributing and carrying out work, just as it applies to progress in any other sphere.

Second, we progressives need to be conscious of the mainspring that underlies our notion of progress. For Voltaire and for many of his 18th century contemporaries the mainspring was the idea of Reason, and progress was progress towards an Age of Reason. Today, two centuries later, the emphasis has changed. Following scientists like Julian Huxley and mystics like Teilhard de Chardin, increasing numbers of us feel that progress is connected with the evolution of consciousness. We feel that social progress is to do with an increase in people's capacity for self-development, and we are coming to see a progressive society as one which positively enables its people and its communities to develop themselves. The mechanistic models of Newtonian science and utilitarian philosophy are losing their energising power as vehicles for the idea of progress. They are being replaced by the developmental models of biology, psychology and evolution. This affects our perception of progress in the sphere of work, as in other spheres.

Third, we progressives should have a clear idea of how progress is to be brought about. If our commitment to progress is practical, then we must see ourselves as practitioners of social change. We need to understand the dynamics of the process of social change, if we are to operate effectively on that process. In this context, Voltaire's position—Tom Paine described him as 'both the flatterer and satirist of despotism'—has relevance for us. Voltaire denounced the heroic tradition in history and philosophy which, as in Machiavelli's thought, focused on the power of princes and put its trust in them. Yet he continued to hope that enlightened despots like Frederick the Great of Prussia would provide the motive force for progress into the Age of Reason. These hopes were not justified, but they were understandable. After all, what practical alternative did there seem to be in mid-18th century Europe?

We run a comparable risk. Increasingly we feel that progress requires us to throw off the domination of big corporations, big government, the mass media, the powerful trade unions, the professional monopolies (for example, in education, medicine and the law), the big money-dealers like banks and building societies—in fact, to liberate ourselves from excessive dependency on the whole complex of formal institutions which make up the over-developed, over-extended modern state. But, at the same time, we find it very difficult to imagine a different context for the reforming (or revolutionary) action which will take us forward. We assume that we need political power, or money, or publicity, or legislation, or professional backing, in order to act effectively; and we are tempted to sink our energies, as Voltaire did, in manipulating the old system in the hope of helping a new one to come to birth.

RIGHTS AND RESPONSIBILITIES

I now want to make three points about rights and responsibilities in general, before coming to the more specific matter of rights and responsibilities connected with work.

I said that we would be wrong to underestimate the constructive contribution which Voltaire made to the mental revolution that preceded the French Revolution. He helped to construct the new set of beliefs that replaced the old assumptions that he had done so much to demolish. And this relates directly to the first point I want to make about rights.

Voltaire's positive contribution to the Enlightenment was to interest his fellow countrymen and women in the thinking of Newton and Locke, and thus to temper the theoretical, deductive rationality of the Cartesian mind with the spirit of English empiricism. The empirical tradition in natural, moral and political philosophy led, of course, to the concepts of natural law and natural rights; and these concepts underlay not only the American Declaration of Independence in 1776 ('we hold these truths to be self-evident') but also the French Declaration of the Rights of Man and of Citizens in 1789. The assumption was that rights existed as part of the natural order, and that by the use of reason we could establish what they were.

Our concept of rights today is more evolutionary. In fact, we see the evolution of rights as an aspect of the evolution of human consciousness. Rights for citizens, the right of slaves to be free, rights for women, rights for members of ethnic minorities, rights for children, rights for animals, rights even for inanimate creatures such as trees—we are now aware of a historical process whereby the treatment of various categories of people or creatures which was deemed acceptable in the past is questioned, is increasingly opposed and repudiated, and is eventually legislated against. This evolutionary nature of rights can be clearly seen in the sphere of employment over the last 150 years.

Second, there is the question of how rights and responsibilities are related. It would be too simple—and too cynical—to define rights as what we claim for ourselves and responsibilities as what we impose on other people. But there does tend to be that kind of asymmetry between the way we think about rights and the way we think about responsibilities. This is, no doubt, due to the fact that, historically, the establishment of rights normally took place in a paternalistic context. The governed established new rights against the governors (or the governors gave new rights to the governed), and the governors accepted responsibility for safeguarding those rights. This tendency to be more concerned about our rights than our responsibilities is fostered in late industrial society by the dominant assumption that we have to look outside ourselves to society's institutions for the meeting of all our needs—to the shops for our food, to the education profession for our learning, to the doctors and the drug industry for our health, to the professional politicians for our politics, to the state for our welfare, to employers for our work. We feel that we have a right to all those things and therefore we feel that the institutions of society have a responsibility to supply them.

In *The Rights of Man* Paine touched on the question of responsibilities, or duties, as follows:

> While the Declaration of Rights was before the National Assembly (in Paris in 1789), some of its members remarked that, if a Declaration of Rights was published, it should be accompanied by a Declaration of Duties. The observation discovered a mind that reflected, and it only erred by not reflecting far enough. A Declaration of Rights is, by reciprocity, a Declaration of Duties also. Whatever is my right as a man, is also the right of another; and it becomes my duty to guarantee it, as well as to possess it.

According to Paine, then, it is my duty or responsibility to guarantee other people's rights—and theirs to guarantee mine. Without wishing to dispute this, we may well feel that Paine himself did not reflect far enough. There is, for example, another sense than his in which responsibilities are reciprocal to rights. Whenever one party is given rights against another, for example an employee against an employer, there are imposed on that other party responsibilities towards the first. If those responsibilities should one day prove infeasible, i.e. impossible to discharge, then the rights which created them will be infeasible too. This is all too relevant for many people in Britain today, in respect of their right to a job.

Moreover, there are two important sets of responsibilities which cannot be defined simply as the reciprocal of rights. One is people's responsibilities to themselves, and the other is responsibilities which people take on themselves. These are perhaps hinted at, though not clearly developed, in Article 29(1) of the Universal Declaration of Human Rights, proclaimed by the United Nations in 1948. This states:

> Everyone has duties to the community in which alone the free and full development of his personality is possible.

This is not far from the notion that people have responsibilities to themselves which no one else can fulfil. That shades into the concept of the right to be responsible. And that, I believe, is now beginning to emerge as one of the energising concepts of our time. The right to be responsible is, of course, directly related to our changing attitudes towards work and to our changing perceptions of what kinds of work are meaningful to us.

My third point follows on. It concerns the internalisation of responsibility. Young children have discipline and control imposed on them by others. As they grow up, they learn—in most cases—to discipline and control themselves. Immature organisations, like profit-making firms, have to have government regulation imposed upon them to ensure they act in socially responsible ways. As they become more mature, they recognise that they do have social responsibilities, and they internalise at least some mechanisms of social self-control. Some business thinkers today believe that big corporations, which now pursue economic goals subject to social constraints, may soon perceive their function differently—as the pursuit of socially useful purposes, subject to the constraints of economic viability and survival. As with growing-up children, and with organisations like business corporations, so with societies. An immature society is one whose members have their values and their responsibilities externally defined and imposed, for example by commercial advertisers and by agencies of government; a mature society is one whose members define their own needs and assume their own responsibilities. The consumer society plus welfare state is, in this reckoning, an immature society in a state of dependency. A more adult society will be one whose members are more self-reliant and more self-responsible.

WORK

Very different attitudes have been, and still are, found towards work. It has been seen, as Voltaire apparently saw it, as an opiate—an activity that makes life bearable. It has been seen as a curse, a punishment by God for Adam's original sin. It has been seen as a blessing, enabling a person to achieve fulfilment. (This blessing idea is questioned by the people of Haiti, who have a proverb: 'If work were a good thing, the rich would have found a way of keeping it for themselves'). Work has been seen as purely instrumental—an activity of no meaning or value to the worker, except insofar as it brings an income. Work has been seen as a social activity, providing a context in which people can relate to one another. Work has been seen as the central core of a person's life, which gives that life its meaning. Work has been seen as something to be avoided at almost any cost—an attitude of well-born people in ancient Greece and Rome which is shared by people we call 'skivers' and 'scroungers' today. Work has been seen as something that most people have to do, but only under compulsion.

These different attitudes toward work reflect different experiences of work, different positions in society, and different cultural backgrounds. Perhaps the main contrast is between people who feel that their work ought to be important and valuable to them, and people who want to reduce to the minimum the role of work in their lives. In this context, a word is needed about the Protestant work ethic and its future.

By attaching a religious and moral value to secular work, the Protestant ethic encouraged entrepreneurs and capitalists to strive for business success, and it encouraged their employees to work for them with a will. To the former it gave moral backing in their struggle to succeed; to the latter it gave moral backing in their struggle to survive. In the course of time it created a situation in which what the world called work became people's main source not only of income but also of social esteem and self-esteem, more or less regardless of the value of the work itself. Today the Protestant ethic has become schismogenic: on the one hand, it makes us feel we ought to have a job—a job being the dominant form of work today; but, on the other hand, it sharpens our awareness that the work done in many jobs today is a futile waste of our time and energy, and in others positively immoral. As the shortage of jobs becomes more severe, the cookie is starting to crumble in two directions. Some people are beginning to decide that work is unimportant after all; they will liberate themselves from the Protestant ethic and devote themselves to other things, such as their family and leisure pursuits. Others are beginning to decide that, because work is so important for them and because good work is so difficult to find in the form of jobs, they will organise their own work for themselves in some other way. These changes of attitude, though apparently opposed to one another, are not so far apart in their practical effects. Both, if they gather momentum, will help to erode the credibility and effectiveness of 'the national labour market', as the main mechanism for distributing work.

This brings us to rights and responsibilities connected with work. Until fairly recently, in fact, it has not been so much a question of rights to work, as of compulsion to work. Much progress has been made in the last, say, 150 years to establish people's rights at work and—at least in theory—the equal rights to work of disadvantaged groups in society. There has also, of course, been a great advance in the rights of working people to organise themselves through trade unions.[3] A measure of this progress can be had by comparing the French Declaration of Rights of Man in 1789, which made no mention of rights to work, with the United Nations Universal Declaration of Human Rights in 1948. This declared, as Article 23:

1. Everyone has the right to work, to free choice of employment, to just and favourable conditions of work and to protection against unemployment.
2. Everyone, without any discrimination, has the right to equal pay for equal work.
3. Everyone who works has the right to just and favourable remuneration, ensuring for himself and his family an existence worthy of human dignity, and supplemented, if necessary, by other means of social protection.
4. Everyone has the right to form and to join trade unions for the protection of his interests.

This advance in people's rights concerning employment, the growth of trade union strength, the development of industrial relations procedures and the extension of legislation to regulate employment is, of course, a huge subject. There is no doubt that these developments have helped to reduce injustice. They have certainly been important. They were probably inevitable. But they are essentially defensive. They belong to a society whose whole historical thrust for the last few hundred years has been to restrict most people's independent right to choose how they will work, and to limit their

[3] [1997 note. Since 1979, in Britain and other countries, the balance of power has swung back to some extent in favour of employers, and organised labour has lost some of its previous rights.]

responsibility for working in accordance with their own perceptions of need and value. It is that right and that responsibility which will, I believe, be most significant for the future.

In feudal times there was the corvée—the day's unpaid work due from a vassal to his lord, which in 18th century France came to mean public labour on the roads. More generally, rents in kind (i.e. some of the fruits of their labour) were due from villeins to their manorial lords. But, as Christopher Hill[4] describes, when the monasteries were dissolved and many great feudal estates were broken up in 16th century England, most of the villeins became landless labourers. The enclosures of the 17th and 18th centuries, which involved the loss of rights to graze cattle, pick up timber, and hunt animals on the common lands, increased their dependence on paid labour. In fact, enclosure of the commons was positively praised by contemporaries because it forced labourers 'to work every day in the year; their children will be put out to labour early'. By depriving the lower orders of any chance of economic independence, 'the subordination of the lower ranks of society would be thereby considerably secured'. Harsh penalties were imposed on the workless poor under the Poor Law from the 16th century, and harsh restrictions on labour mobility under laws such as the great Statute of Artificers of 1563. These made doubly sure that people who had no property would have no escape route from a semi-servile state and their 'duty to work for their betters', and that a pool of cheap labour would always be available for employers.

The coming of the factory system brought a further deprivation of independence at work. E. P. Thompson describes its impact on the life of weavers:

> Weaving had offered an employment to the whole family, even when spinning was withdrawn from the home. The young children winding bobbins, older children watching for faults, picking over the cloth, or helping to throw the shuttle in the broad-loom; adolescents working a second or third loom; the wife taking a turn at weaving in and among her domestic employments. The family was together, and however poor meals were, at least they could sit down at chosen times. A whole pattern of family and community life had grown up around the loom-shops; work did not prevent conversation or singing. The spinning-mills—which offered employment only for their children—and then the power-loom shed which generally employed only the wives or adolescents— were resisted until poverty broke down all defences.[5]

Most people today, nearly 200 years later, are conditioned to take for granted that work has little connection with any pattern of family and community life.

[4] Christopher Hill, *Reformation to Industrial Revolution*, Penguin, 1969. See especially pp. 57 and 270.

[5] E. P. Thompson, *The Making of the English Working Class*, Penguin, 1968. See p. 339.

It has not occurred to many of us until quite recently that men as well as women might have a right, or perhaps even feel a responsibility, to work directly for and in our families and communities. The pressures pushing people towards employment unconnected with family or community have been very strong. They include: the reduction in the number of small firms and small farms; the inflation of property prices, making it difficult for most people to buy land; personnel management procedures which discourage part-time employment; pension practices which discourage early retirement from employment; social security procedures which encourage unemployed people (including, for example, single parents) to seek employment; and trade union pressures which seek to reserve work for full-time employees. Only in the last few years, as the prospects of restoring and maintaining permanent full employment have become bleaker, have attempts been made to proclaim new rights in respect of work—such as the right to work in socially useful ways,[6] the right to useful unemployment,[7] and the right to leisure.[8]

However, I believe we may now be near a turning point. It is becoming apparent that full employment was a transient phenomenon, belonging uniquely to that period of 25 years or so after the Second World War, which marked the climax of the industrial age. In the last few years, as the national labour market has begun to break down and lose its credibility as a mechanism for distributing society's work, more and more people have begun to think about what 'post-industrial' arrangements may take its place. A widening range of practical initiatives and projects have been launched which create new contexts for work.

The following changes are likely to be among the most important. Together they could combine to ease the unemployment problem very significantly. The key is that they help to provide solutions to today's employment problems which are also stepping stones to new patterns of work for the future.

First, the revival of local economies is now a top priority in many parts of the industrialised world. Large numbers of local communities and towns are threatened by the decline of industries (like steel or ship-building or textiles or nickel-mining or railways or motor-manufacturing) on which they have become all too dependent for employment. As central governments and national and multi-national employers prove less and less willing and able to

---

[6] [1997 note. For the Lucas Aerospace Shopstewards Combine Committee's campaign to work on socially useful products, see chapter 3, footnote 5.]

[7] Ivan Illich, *The Right to Useful Unemployment,* Marion Boyars, 1978.

[8] A right to expanded and regular leisure was proposed by Clive Jenkins and Barry Sherman, *The Collapse of Work,* Eyre Methuen, 1979.

bail them out, people living in these places are realising that the revival of local economies and of local employment is something that will have to be initiated locally if it is going to happen at all. They are starting to explore the scope for providing more local work by meeting more of their own basic needs locally, for example by growing more of their food and by substituting local energy sources for imports of electricity and other forms of fuel and power from elsewhere. Not only in this country but also in places like Sudbury in Canada and Jamestown in the United States, local enterprise trusts, citizens' groups, community enterprises, common ownerships, co-operatives, county energy plans and other local initiatives are now springing up, and local centres of knowledge and skill (like colleges) and local associations (like trades councils and chambers of commerce) are beginning to get into the act.[9]

Second, not just the locality but also the household may once again become an important centre for production and work, as it was before the industrial age drove work out of the home into factories and offices and other institutions like hospitals and schools. Miniaturised technology—including the microprocessor and other electronic technology such as micro-computers, video terminals and word-processors—will make it possible to do at home much of the work now done in factories and offices. People who handle information, like computer programmers and insurance salespeople, are moving in this direction already. At the same time, increasing numbers of people are already spending more time on DIY (do-it-yourself) and other informal kinds of work for themselves, their families, and their friends and neighbours. Food growing is one example. Car maintenance, plumbing, electrical work, carpentry and various aspects of home maintenance are others. Moonlighting, legal and illegal, is on the increase. As this continues, and as arrangements for exchanging skills and services with neighbours outside the formal labour market continue to spread, this will stimulate the further growth of productive work in and around the home.

Third, our changing attitudes to men's work and women's work may be especially significant. As the industrial way of life developed in the 18th and 19th centuries, men's work and women's work diverged and the split between

[9] [1997 note. Interest in local economic regeneration and self-reliance has continued to grow throughout the 1980s and 1990s. It has been reflected in transnational programmes under the auspices of the European Commission and the OECD. (David Cadman and I did a study on finance for local employment initiatives for both those organisations in 1984/5.) But economic policy-makers and commentators have continued to see local economies as peripheral to mainstream economic issues. Richard Douthwaite, *Short Circuit: Strengthening Local Economies for Security in an Unstable World*, Green Books, 1996 is a good practical guide for local communities which can no longer rely on the global and national economy to provide the necessities of life.]

them became more marked. The father became the breadwinner going out to work for money, while the mother became the housewife staying at home. Because industrialised society increased the importance of money in people's lives, the paid work of men acquired a higher status than the unpaid work of women—although women's work was always more closely concerned with basic human needs. This led to the women's movement insisting that women should have more equal employment rights with men, and women now have a fairer deal so far as paid work is concerned. But progress has been lop-sided, and men do not yet undertake their fair share of the unpaid work of running the household and raising the family. But they are becoming aware that they tend to miss out on these convivial, familial, neighbourly aspects of life. This could be a crucial trigger for change. Men's attitudes to work could alter sooner than many people think, under growing pressure from their women-folk, a growing shortage of full-time jobs, and a growing sense that much men's work in factories, offices and the professions is socially useless and personally arid.

This would contribute, fourth, to a rapidly spreading demand for part-time jobs among men as well as women. Opening up new opportunities for part-time jobs would enable more people, regardless of their sex, both to earn an income and to have more time to spend on voluntary work, family-raising, and DIY in and around their homes. Job-sharing, longer holidays, shorter working hours, and earlier retirement could merge with part-time jobs to provide a wider variety of working patterns from which people could choose the way of working that suits them best. For some people a part-time job could provide a stepping stone to self-employment. In all these ways the spread of part-time jobs could help to leave more jobs and employment opportunities available for the many people (including young people and handicapped people) whose claim to be provided with a job is particularly strong, because they cannot reasonably be expected to organise work for themselves.

CONCLUSION

Let me now try to draw the threads together.

First, then, we are living, as Voltaire was living, at a time when a transformation of our society cannot be far off. Its dominant institutions have become absurdly overdeveloped, and we have become absurdly dependent on them. In no aspect of our lives is this more significant than in the sphere of work.

Secondly, we are living through a time when progress in establishing many new rights has, paradoxically, diminished our effective right to take responsibility for ourselves. As the institutions of modern society, such as the national labour market, become less able to deliver the goods we require of them, such as jobs, we shall find it necessary to take more responsibility to ourselves.

Thirdly, for several hundred years forces have been strongly at work in our society which have tended to deprive most people of an effective right to define for themselves, in accordance with their own needs and values, how they should use (and develop) their own capacity for work. One of the most exciting possibilities now confronting us is of a change of direction in this respect.

As and when we bring this change about (and we will have to take the initiative ourselves, not try to get the government and other institutions to do it for us), we shall open up the prospect of good work for many more people than have enjoyed it in the past. By 'good work' I mean what E. F. Schumacher[10] meant. First, it is work that provides necessary goods and services; it meets needs. Second, it is work that enables people to use and develop their abilities and aptitudes and experience; it contributes to human growth. Third, it is work done in service to and in co-operation with other people, thus liberating us from the limits of egocentricity; it contributes to the growth of people as social beings.

Good work, in short, contributes to self-development and the evolution of consciousness. Henceforth good work will be an essential part of progress. It requires that we claim and exercise the right to be responsible.

Ironbridge, Shropshire
1980

[10] E. F. Schumacher, *Good Work*, Cape, 1979.

5

After the Welfare State

This chapter is based on a paper originally given at a conference on 'Welfarism—What Now?' organised by Nordal Akerman for the Swedish Committee for Future Oriented Research in Stockholm in August 1980, and later published in *Futures*, in February 1982.

The paper was written following an attachment to the University of Calgary, Alberta, arranged by Tim Tyler, Dean of the Faculty of Social Welfare. It was one of the outcomes of a project on 'Changing Direction' sponsored by:

- Continuing Management Education Programme, Loughborough University (Gurth Higgin);
- Intermediate Technology Development Group (John Davis and George McRobie);
- International Foundation for Social Innovation, Paris (Georges Gueron);
- Joseph Rowntree Charitable Trust (Grigor McClelland);
- Scott Bader Commonwealth (Godric Bader); and
- the Vanier Institute for the Family, Ottawa (Bill Dyson).

As published in *Futures*, the paper began with an account of the HE and SHE visions of the future, and of the nature of the change of direction to a SHE path of future development. That part of the paper has been left out here to avoid duplication with earlier chapters.

January 1997

What Comes After the Welfare State?
A Post-Welfare Development Path for the UK

Richard Titmuss[1] described the social services as 'an integral part of industrialisation'. They are the mode of providing for social welfare that industrial society has evolved following the breakdown of the old social fabric during and after the Industrial Revolution. Now industrial society in its turn has reached the limit of its development path and is nearing breakdown. The whole constellation of assumptions (the paradigm) on which industrial society has evolved, and on which its institutions and the relationships between them are based, is rapidly losing its capacity to energise, to justify and to explain. We therefore face a change of direction in the development of social welfare, as of everything else.

The question, 'what comes after the Welfare State?' implies that we cannot develop the Welfare State further on lines envisaged by the hyper-expansionists, and equally that we cannot go back to the bad old pre-welfare days of early industrial society. We are seeking ways forward into a truly post-industrial future in which people will be better able, and be better enabled, to create welfare for themselves and one another—what the Vanier Institute calls a 'more familial' society.

Many thinkers about social policy and many practitioners of social administration are already coming to grips with this challenge, and are placing new emphasis on voluntary social service and self-help. I hope some of them may find encouragement and stimulus in this chapter.

THE INDUSTRIAL PARADIGM

The industrial paradigm embraces the following interrelated assumptions:

- progress consists in separating the economic and social aspects of life;
- progress consists in separating the activities of production and consumption;
- progress consists in specialisation;
- progress consists in the formalisation (including monetisation,

---

[1] Richard Titmuss, *Essays on the Welfare State*, George Allen and Unwin, London, 1963.

institutionalisation and professionalisation) of the production of
goods and provision of services; and
- the growth of social welfare depends on the growth of economic
prosperity which must, therefore, be given priority.

20th century socialists have shared these assumptions with 19th century
radical capitalists. Just as the latter assumed in the 1830s that solutions to the
'condition of England question' depended on the stimulus to economic
activity that free trade and retrenchment of government spending would
provide, so the latter—like C. A. R. Crosland in *The Future of Socialism*[2]—
assumed that economic growth was an essential prerequisite to increasing
social welfare. The same, of course, is true of US multinational business
tycoons and Soviet state planners today.

There was a recent period, during the 'Butskellite' consensus[3] of the
1950s, when mature industrial society in the UK seemed to most people to be
progressing more or less satisfactorily according to these assumptions. But
this was not long sustained. On the one hand the limits to economic growth
began to close in, while on the other the demand for social welfare services—
fed by their availability at public expense, by widening perceptions of the scale
of social need that ought to be met, by the vested interest of the growing
number of social service professionals, and by the general readiness of
politicians to offer more—began to escalate. The industrial growth engine
turned, in a few short years, from a miracle machine capable of meeting
continually growing needs into a disaster device programmed to generate
aspirations which it could not possibly fulfil—and programmed, moreover, to
stunt people's capacity to fulfil their aspirations for themselves.

Conventional politicians of all shades in the UK today (including Mrs
Thatcher and Sir Keith Joseph who believe in the invisible hand of the market
economy, the left-wing Bennite socialists who believe in the omnicompetence
of a benign state, and those in between—social democrats, liberals and 'wet'
conservatives—who believe in a mixed economy) still cling to the industrial
paradigm. They continue to assume that economic recovery on conventional
lines is prerequisite to the provision of increased social welfare on
conventional lines, and the main argument between them is about how
economic recovery is to be achieved. They will continue to voice this basic set
of assumptions, though with declining conviction and credibility, until others
have articulated clearly and coherently a new set of assumptions to succeed it.
To articulate that new set of assumptions is one of the most important tasks
of the present creative, pre-political phase of the transition to a post-

[2] C. A. R. Crosland, *The Future of Socialism*, Cape, London, 1956.
[3] From the names of R. A. Butler (Conservative) and Hugh Gaitskell (Labour).

industrial society.[4]

The whole thrust of industrial progress has been to drive human activity out of the informal sector (in which the economic and social, and for that matter cultural, aspects of life were closely intertwined) into the formal sector (where social became separated from economic activity and consumption from production, where more and more activities became professionalised, and where economists could count the money value of what happened). The institutionalised activities of society became, with industrialisation, so dominant that questions about the operation of the formal economy and the organised social services became the only economic and social issues considered worthy of debate by politicians and serious commentators. The change of direction to a post-welfare development path must involve a revitalisation of the informal sector, in which the separation between economic and social activities, between production and consumption, and between the life of the household and the life of the local community, will no longer be so sharp as it has become during the industrial age.

Meanwhile, the centralisation of political and economic power has become an increasingly dominant trend in late industrial society; this has provoked a 'small is beautiful' backlash; and the 'vertical' conflict between centralisation and decentralisation, big and small, has now emerged as a rival dimension of political choice to the conventional 'horizontal' choices of right, left and centre. An important aspect of the post-industrial future will be a revitalisation of local control over economic and social, as well as political, affairs—or, to put it more exactly, a reintegration of economic, social and political autonomy at the local level.

These perspectives suggest two main features of the SHE approach to the future of social welfare (as to the future of economic wellbeing and of employment and work): first, more and more people should be enabled to become more self-reliant in their homes and families, and to participate more actively as members of their local communities; second, more and more local communities should be enabled likewise to achieve more economic, social and political autonomy and to become more active participants in the economic, social and political life of the wider society of which they are part.

Let me emphasise that this approach differs diametrically from the HE vision of post-industrial society, one of whose main features is the growth of dependency on centralised technocracy and professionalised services. I do not

[4] I clearly recall that, at an international conference organised by Alison Pritchard and myself at Hawkwood near Stroud in the spring of 1979, Bill Dyson impressed on me that creative thinking and dissemination of ideas about social transformation belonged, not to the processes and activities of mainstream politics, but to pre-political processes and activities aimed at getting new ideas and new policies on to the mainstream political agenda.

see how that could possibly be a desirable or feasible path into the future. It implies that people should be seen as a problem, not a resource. It implies a society increasingly split between managerial technocracy and dependent clientele. I am not saying this is far-fetched. In Sweden, for example, it has been calculated that, if the social services continue to develop in the same way as hitherto, in a few decades half the population will be employed taking care of the other half.[5] But a future which implies a continuing expansion of people's needs and of their incapacity to meet those needs for themselves and one another—a continuing growth of alienation and perceived helplessness—cannot be sustainable for long.[6]

THE KEY DILEMMA: PERSONS OR SOCIETY?

The future of welfare raises directly the crucial dilemma that faces all who propose a transformation of society: should we first try to change people (including ourselves) or first try to change society? The dilemma is that, unless we become better people, we will be unable to create a better society; whereas unless we create a better society, the existing social environment will prevent us from becoming better people.

Welfare services and social policy range from personal counselling, through the administration of welfare benefits and services, to community development and radical social action. There has been much debate about which end of the spectrum is more important. Is there a conflict between them? Should we help people to function better in society as it is? Or should we change society for the better?

This question—which comes first, persons or society?—affects most areas of social policy. Here are three examples among many. First, is poverty due to personal laziness and lack of willpower, or to the injustice of society? A recent survey[7] showed that in the UK we tend to blame people for being poor, whereas other Europeans tend to blame society for people's poverty. Second, in order to improve health, should we encourage people personally to refrain from too much drink, tobacco, and junkfood? Or should we try to change the policies of the institutions—the industries, the advertising media, and the Treasury—which depend for their revenue on high sales of these products? Third, is social work that helps people to cope with the problems of

---

[5] *Care in Society*, 1979, a project presentation by the Secretariat for Future Studies, Stockholm.

[6] [1997 note. It has now become clear that the once admired Swedish welfare state is, in fact, not financially sustainable.]

[7] *The Perception of Poverty in Europe*, Commision of the European Communities, rue de la Loi, 1049 Brussels, Belgium.

poverty, unemployment, ill-health, etc., the right approach? Or is it, as many radicals argue, merely a control function performed for the governing classes to socialise working-class people into the existing economic system?

I argued in *The Sane Alternative* that we have to find ways of transcending this person/society dilemma. So far as we ourselves are concerned, we have to find ways of acting which simultaneously change our own way of living and help to change the way society functions—in other words, ways of acting and being which contribute at the same time to our own development as persons-in-society and to the development of a more person-centred society. Recent initiatives by the Association of Humanistic Psychology have this aim clearly in view. So far as other people are concerned, we have to find ways of helping them which at the same time help to create a new direction for society. These will be ways, especially, of enabling people to help themselves and by doing so to help to change society around them. Consciousness-raising is often directed to this. In general, the way out of the dilemma is to look for solutions to the problems of people today which will at the same time be stepping stones towards a new society tomorrow.

As we pursue the practicalities of the post-welfare development path, the links between personal development, social service and social action will be of the greatest importance. If we ignore them there will always be a risk that personal development may degenerate into narcissism, that social service may degenerate into new forms of domination and dependency-creation, and that political and social action may degenerate into an outlet for the displaced personal growth needs of the activists concerned.

SELF-DEVELOPMENT FOR PERSONS AND COMMUNITIES

A central concept, then, for the post-welfare development path will be self-development for persons and communities; and the link between the two will attract increasing attention.

In many practical ways this is already evident. The growing interest in local enterprise trusts, decentralised energy strategy, community health centres and other approaches to local community development is matched by the growing interest in the kinds of education and training that enable people to develop their individual skills and capacities—whether practical (like plumbing and gardening), personal (like meditation), or interpersonal (like counselling). All this is a vital part of the post-welfare development path. But in the present context I wish to discuss a developmental possibility more directly related to the welfare approach.

The interest in personal therapies (that help people to deal with problems perceived as damaging) and personal growth techniques (that help people to tap their potential for a better life) has grown significantly in recent years. (In practice, the dividing line between therapies and growth techniques is blurred.) How far may it be possible to develop generally applicable community therapies and community growth techniques on similar lines? And, further, how far may it be possible to make explicit the link between community growth and the personal growth of people living in the community concerned?

As an example of a personal therapy I take the Heimler Scale of Social Functioning. In *Survival in Society*[8] Eugene Heimler asks how we can turn the welfare state concept into a concept of self-help, and describes an approach based on the use of his scale. The scale is comprised of the three indices set out below, which he calls 'positive', 'negative', and 'synthesis':

- The positive index asks five questions on each of the following five topics: finance; sex; primary and secondary family relationships; friendship; work and/or outside interests. The responses can be positive, negative or uncertain, scoring 4, 0, and 2 respectively.
- The negative index is designed to indicate the nature of frustration. It asks five questions on each of the following topics: activity; somatic; personal; depression; escape routes. Again the scoring is 4, 0, and 2.
- The synthesis scale evaluates past, present and future aspirations. It asks five questions (e.g. 'How far have you achieved your ambition in life?'), each of which is scored between 0 and 20 (e.g. 'not at all' and 'completely').

The scale thus generates a profile for each person who, as an integral part of his or her therapy, completes the questionnaire. Its primary use is to provide people, in discussion with the therapist, with starting points for action to improve their social functioning. Its value as a device for enabling people to see how they can help themselves appears unquestionable. (It can also be used by therapists diagnostically; to measure improvement; to indicate priority cases for treatment; and to give warning of possibilities, e.g. of suicide.)

Much information is now becoming available about community economic development, local enterprise trusts, participatory planning, anticipatory democracy, and other approaches to local self-development, including community health, community education, community arts, and community communications. Sudbury (Canada), Jamestown (USA),

[8] Eugene Heimler, *Survival in Society*, Weidenfeld and Nicolson, London, 1975. Heimler is Professor of Social Functioning at Calgary University. He is also Chairman of the Institute of Social Functioning in England.

Craigmillar (Scotland) and Altrincham (England) are among many localities where various methods of animating community decision making and stimulating public discussion of local futures have recently been documented. As it becomes necessary in more and more localities to accelerate the change of direction to a post-welfare development path, techniques analogous to the Heimler Scale of Social Functioning for individuals, will need to be validated and brought into widespread use to animate community consciousness and to enable local communities to evolve new perceptions of community needs, community potential, and possible courses of community action. What is required is a generally applicable framework which would enable communities to establish a profile for themselves of perceived needs, perceived satisfactions and perceived frustrations (in areas like employment, transport, welfare, health, education, and so on), as a basis on which to mobilise energy for purposeful community action. An example may be a 'social balance sheet for the town' (*bilan social de la ville*) which is drawn up, using a process of public participation, under the headings Housing, Education, Culture, Leisure, Health, Security, Communication, Administration, Production, Distribution, and Solidarity. The suggestion is that drawing up this social balance sheet every five years could become a regular part of the planning process.

POST-WELFARE ROLE OF PROFESSIONALS

A vital task for professionals, as we switch to the post-welfare development path, will be to help persons and communities to become more self-reliant and to acquire the capacity for self-development—for example, by offering the kind of technique which I have just discussed, and knowing from experience how it can be successfully used. People from many different professional backgrounds—engineers, planners, builders, architects, managers, accountants, even economists—will have much to offer, and welfare professionals will be among them.

Even without this new task, I would not argue, as some do, that we ought to get rid of professions and professional people altogether. In social welfare, as in other spheres, professionally trained and experienced people will continue to have an important remedial, trouble-shooting role. Sick and injured people will need doctors and medical care. Disabled and poor people will need the support of social services. Distressed people will need help. Social emergencies will always occur, and they will have to be dealt with.

At the same time there is no doubt that the professions, including the welfare professions, are today in crisis. The arm's length relationship between professional and client is often found to be less conducive to the client's well-being than sympathetic personal care. The increasing professionalisation of social service is seen to turn the recipients of care into dependent consumers of welfare and to reduce their capacity to create well-being for themselves.

Because people's problems provide professionals with material to work on and a livelihood, they tend to be defined to match the skills and experience that the professionals have acquired. Problems that professionals happen to find exciting, such as organ transplants in medicine, receive a disproportionate amount of attention compared with others which may affect the well-being of many more people.

Demarcation lines between professions mean that people are dealt with as bundles of technical problems rather than as whole people. Demarcation disputes and rivalries between professions can create gratuitous problems for people needing care. In general, professionals in the social and caring fields are finding it increasingly necessary to compromise between their responsibility to their employers, their responsibility to their clients or patients, their responsibility to their professional colleagues, and their responsibility to society at large.

These problems are now well recognised. Of even greater importance, perhaps, is the fact that in their existing role the remedial professions cannot create conditions which positively foster well-being. The medical and health professions can help to remedy ill health; they may even sometimes contribute to measures which help to prevent it; but they can do little to create conditions which positively foster good health. Those derive from the ways we treat ourselves, one another and our environment (sanely, humanely, and ecologically—or otherwise), and from activities and policies right outside the sphere of the medical and health professionals.

Similarly, social workers can help to deal with social problems once the problems have occurred; but they cannot help to create the patterns of residential, working and leisure life that will positively generate social wellbeing. Those derive from activities and policies right outside the social workers' sphere. Lawyers can do little to create a more law-abiding society. Even professional educators, though most of them are not explicitly involved in remedial work, have little opportunity or capacity—schooled and organised as they are to operate within the closed confines of the education system—to help to create a society that is more conducive to learning. The priority that people give to developing their knowledge and skills, and the effect of their lifestyle and environment on their capacity to learn, is determined by economic, social and cultural factors outside the professional educators' sphere.

The post-welfare challenge, then—to enable persons and communities to acquire the capacity for self-reliance and self-development—may, as an incidental bonus, turn out to offer a solution to the present problems of the professions, and a way out of the crisis which they now face. The practical questions are many. For example, how will professionals learn the experience and skills to help people and communities to develop themselves? How will members of different professions—planners, social workers, public health workers, community development workers, energy experts, employment officials, social security officials, etc.—find ways of working together to contribute to the self-development of their local community? But once the overall aim, the new paradigm, is clearly and simply accepted, these practical questions will find practical answers.

SOME PROBLEMS

No one should, however, suppose that changing direction will be easy. The obstacles will include: resistance by people with a vested interest in the status quo; organisational incapacity for change; personal incapacity for change; and the propensity to co-opt new initiatives into supporting the old patterns of being and doing.

The enabling approach will be resisted by people who, because of their vested interests, their institutional and professional role, or their personal temperament, wish to keep other people dependent on them and preserve their own position and sense of superiority. As the industrialised way of life continues to break down, necessity will compel increasing numbers of such people to accept change, and the more far-sighted will positively embrace the widening opportunities to 'decolonise' the old system. But, although the diehards will eventually die out, as have most of the blimps who struggled to preserve the British Empire, they will need to be confronted and defeated meanwhile.

The institutional capabilities we have inherited from the industrial age do not equip us for the tasks of enabling. Structurally, the administration of social policy has developed separately from economic policy. Local government's responsibilities for social services have not been matched by corresponding powers and responsibilities for local economic development or local employment. In central government, responsibilities for social and economic policies have been split between different departments. To take one example, social security payments from the state to the citizen have been handled by a social services department, whereas tax payments from citizen to the state have been the responsibility of the Inland Revenue, an economic department. So, although a restructuring of the whole system of taxation and social security (including its devolution to local control, at least in part) will be an important aspect of the enabling approach, no persons or organisations currently exist with the skill, the will, or the authority to work out how this restructuring should be done. I do not yet see what practical steps can be taken to remedy this, without leading us into the trap of fruitless institutional reform in which so many of us wasted our energies during the 1960s and 1970s.

Our personal capacities for productive community relationships have also been stunted by the industrial age, which has established a market in labour, and has monetised human activity. As Karl Polanyi pointed out,[9] this has led to the replacement of organic forms of social relations by individualistic forms of economic organisation, or—in the terms I use—informal economic activity has been replaced by formal economic activity. The industrial ethos has tended to destroy non-contractual relations between persons. It is now difficult for mutually supportive social relations to reform spontaneously. We have learned to impute a monetary value to what we do for other people and what they do for us, thus undermining our capacity for mutually supportive social relations.

The approach to personal and community self-development discussed in this paper will help to overcome these problems. So may the growing number of actual examples. Many people and groups in the UK are already working in one field or another to foster greater self-reliance for persons, communities and localities. The value of such examples is threefold. First, they can provide specific illustration for an otherwise general discussion. Second, examples can fortify lonely pioneers in the knowledge that they are not alone on the new development path. Third, an initiative already taken in one place may sometimes to some extent be replicable elsewhere, thus speeding the learning process.

But too much concern for examples may prove to be a trap. First, no example can prove the feasibility of a new development path. Whether a particular initiative is succeeding or failing, or whether it genuinely represents a change of direction toward a new future or is merely a fringe activity parasitical on today's socioeconomic system, is always open to argument by the sceptical. Such argument will distract energies that could be used more profitably. The second danger is more insidious. The whole range of activities involved in compiling, studying, researching, analysing, assessing, evaluating, criticising and discussing, but not taking part in, what other people are trying to do, is typical of late industrial society. If we genuinely want to go down the post-welfare development path towards a SHE society, we should be more

---

[9] Karl Polanyi, *The Great Transformation*, Octagon Books, New York, reprinted 1975.

concerned with how we propose to act ourselves than with discussing the activities of others. The conversion of the efforts of a comparatively small number of social innovators and entrepreneurs into material for study and evaluation by a comparatively large number of researchers, analysts, academics and functionaries is an instance of the propensity to co-opt of which we should beware.

CONCLUSIONS

Serious, practical initiatives are now needed to create a successor to the Welfare State. I have sketched some of the background and indicated some basic problems, and suggested that a key concept for the post-welfare development path will be self-development for persons and communities, outlining throughout a few of the issues that seem likely to be important. I would now like to make my concluding comments.

Along with increasing numbers of other people, I share the view that the right development path for today's industrialised countries will involve:

- a bigger economic role for households and neighbourhoods;
- a more self-sufficient, decentralised economy;
- a new role for unpaid work;
- the possibility that unemployment benefit (and other social payments) could become a recognised source of money income for people doing useful unpaid work in and around their home and neighbourhood;
- a new distribution of paid and unpaid work between men and women;
- higher esteem for caring, people-centred occupations of the kinds traditionally regarded as women's work in the home and neighbourhood, as compared with traditional forms of men's work dealing with things, papers and ideas in factories, offices and universities; and
- forms of continuing education which will bring children, adults, and the elderly closer together in contexts of shared relevance.

These changes will be directly linked with others in the spheres of technology, industry, agriculture, employment, politics and government. They will also be directly linked with changes in the sphere of social welfare, social policy and social administration, with which this paper has been particularly concerned.

I would like to conclude with a list of some of the specific issues which now need to be pursued:

85

- What steps can be taken which, by helping to revitalise the informal economy, will encourage people to enter into mutually supportive social relations? What existing discouragements need to be removed? What changes, for example, in the tax and social security system would help? What changes, again, may be needed to give families and communities improved access to capital and land?
- How might more supportive social relations evolve into, or merge with new forms of organised socio-economic activity?
- Can aids to community self-development be based on a 'scale of social functioning' for communities analogous, for example, to the Heimler Scale of Social Functioning for persons?
- In what other practical ways can links be encouraged between the movement for personal development and the movement for community development?
- As a step towards establishing mutually supportive social relation, can professionals from different specialisms in the social and planning fields be brought together to explore the links between the self-development of their clients and other persons in their communities, and the development of those communities as a whole?
- How can progressive thinkers and radical activists in the social welfare sphere be brought together more often with their opposite numbers in spheres like community enterprise, appropriate technology and local economic development to explore the practicalities of a post-welfare development path?

Ironbridge, Shropshire

1980

6

A New Politics

This chapter was published as the Introduction to the British edition of Fritjof Capra and Charlene Spretnak, *Green Politics: The Global Promise*, (Hutchinson, 1984).

Since 1984, environmental issues have gained much greater attention in political debate and public policy making generally. But this has not been accompanied by a corresponding improvement in the fortunes of green political parties. That is due, at least partly, to considerations mentioned in this chapter. Those remain valid, as it seems to me, in spite of the political changes that have taken place since the chapter was written.

Among the most important of those changes, as will be apparent to readers of this chapter now, have been the collapse of the Soviet systems of government and economy in Russia and Eastern Europe, and the unification of East and West Germany. But these do not, I would argue, call in question the suggestion that 'the politics of constructive social change can often be most effectively pursued outside the realm of conventional political activity'. That, after all, was how the Soviet system was finally brought down. When the 'Reformation' of globalised free-market capitalism eventually takes place, it may happen in a similar way.

January 1997

Introduction to *Green Politics: The Global Promise*

The dominant forms of politics and government throughout the world today are based on mass political parties and centralised bureaucracies. They reflect the factory mentality of the industrial age. This is no less true of the parliamentary democracies of the western world than of the Marxist systems of government in Russia, Eastern Europe and other socialist countries. Looking back, for example to the middle ages, we see that our contemporary forms of politics and government replaced earlier forms that also matched the patterns of activity, structures of society, and cultural and religious beliefs, of their times. Just so, looking forward as the industrial age comes to an end, we can see that in their turn today's ways of doing politics and government will inevitably be replaced by new ones. The new ways of doing politics and governing ourselves will match the new patterns of activity, new structures of society and new systems of beliefs prevalent in the next historical period—the next stage of human development—that is now due.

The Greens in West Germany have achieved worldwide recognition for their political successes in the last few years. In *Green Politics* Fritjof Capra and Charlene Spretnak describe these, together with the problems that the Greens have encountered. They discuss comparable developments in other countries, and place them in a global context. They explore the forms which Green politics could take in the United States. As their book makes very clear, the issues raised by the rise of Green politics, and in particular by the achievements of the German Greens, are deeply significant for the future.

These issues have their own particular relevance for Britain. So, although hitherto I have not specifically thought of myself as a 'Green', I was delighted when the authors invited me to introduce *Green Politics* to British readers.

Growing numbers of people all over the world now firmly believe that the transition to the post-industrial age—or however else we prefer to describe the period of history now beginning—will involve a transformation of our existing way of life in all its aspects, and that such a transformation has indeed already begun. The way we live, work, organise our societies, think of ourselves in relation to other people and the universe around us—all these will change just as deeply as they changed in the course of the Industrial Revolution in the eighteenth and nineteenth centuries. This time the change will involve a shift of emphasis away from means towards ends; away from economic growth towards human development; away from quantitative towards qualitative values and goals; away from the impersonal and organisational towards the personal and interpersonal; and away from the earning and spending of money towards the meeting of real human needs and aspirations. A culture that has been masculine, aggressive and domineering in its outlook will give place to one which is more feminine, co-operative and supportive. A culture that has exalted the uniformly European will give place to one which values the multi-cultural richness and diversity of human experience. An anthropocentric worldview that has licensed the human species to exploit the rest of nature as if from above and outside it, will give place to an ecological worldview. We shall recognise that survival and self-realisation alike require us to act as what we really are—integral parts of an ecosystem much larger, more complex and more powerful than ourselves.

Countless initiatives in many countries are now giving expression to the fact that this transformation is getting under way. Among them are the feminist movement, the environmental movement, the soft energy movement, the holistic health movement, the organic farming movement, the animal rights movement, the decentralist and bioregional movements, the growing demand for greater economic self-reliance at local levels, and the pressures now building up for a fundamental change in the organisation and purposes of work in the post-industrial age.

Those of us who are involved in these initiatives are always faced with a dilemma: should we try to work in and with the established organisations and professions concerned with the matters in question (e.g. the medical establishment in the case of holistic health)? Or is it more realistic to assume that the established structures and processes are irretrievably committed to the *status quo*, and therefore that we should work outside them and even against them? There are arguments for and against both courses. What actually happens is that some of us decide one way, and others the other. Some work to achieve reform from within the established structures and processes. Others work outside, trying to create situations which we hope will force the established institutions to respond, or trying to create new initiatives and new ways of doing things which will encroach upon and perhaps eventually replace the established institutions. It may often be difficult for insiders and outsiders, each working in our own ways for change, to co-operate explicitly with one another. But our activities often complement and reinforce one another, nonetheless.

The dilemma arises with particular force in the context of politics. In trying to achieve the changes we seek, should we do so through the established political processes? Or should we work outside them?

1984 A New Politics

On the one hand, we who live in late industrial societies have learned to think of the processes of politics and government as centrally important. We have become accustomed to think of government as the main instrument of social change, or as the main obstacle to it, and sometimes simultaneously as both; we see politics as the main way to influence the actions of government. We cannot simply turn our back on the opportunities that political involvement seems to offer for helping to shape the kind of future we want. To do so simply because of the difficulties would be sheer escapism. On the other hand, the institutions and processes of politics and government as they exist today are part and parcel of the past which is on the way out—patriarchal, exploitative, adversarial, centralised, unecological. They cannot but distort the issues they deal with, by casting them in obsolescent categories of perception, debate and action. If we commit our energies to politics as politics is understood today, not only may we find our effort to create a new future rejected and ourselves represented as freakish outsiders for making the effort at all. We may also find that involvement in conventional politics positively diminishes our own capacity for constructive thought and action. It may confine us in a sterile—i.e. patriarchal, exploitative, adversarial, etc.— cast of thought and action. It may weaken our ability to work together in creative co-operation with our fellows, whom we may come to perceive as competitors for attention and power. It may compel us to compromise with other political groups, and so obscure the clarity of our message. Moreover, just by sinking our energies in conventional politics, we may be helping to reinforce their credibility. As the sticker says, 'Don't vote. It only encourages them.'

Green Politics shows how issues of this kind have arisen for the German Greens, and how the German Greens have handled them. For example, it describes their need to reconcile the diverse orientations of different types of Greens—visionary/holistic Greens, environmentalist Greens, peace-movement Greens and radical-left Greens; also it discusses the conflicts that have arisen between 'fundamental oppositionists' and 'realists' ('*fundis*' and '*realos*') when the question of coalition with other political parties has come up. In such matters as these—and perhaps especially on the difficult question of co-operation between Greens and Reds, i.e. ecologists and radical socialists—people in other countries can learn valuable lessons from the experience of the West German Greens. Moreover, I believe that people in other countries can profit from the lessons that Charlene Spretnak and Fritjof Capra have drawn about the future of Green politics in the United States.

However, as they point out, the context differs from one country to another. No one country can provide a model for another. In assessing the particular relevance for Britain of the experience of the West German Greens,

91

we have to recognise that the British context differs from the West German one in two important respects.

On the one hand, the West German political system is more open than ours in Britain. For a start, it is more decentralised. Many of the powers exercised by the national Parliament and government in Britain are exercised in West Germany at the level of the regional states (the Länder). Even more significant, the West German electoral system is based on proportional representation, and new parties there begin to win seats in the national, state, or local legislature as soon as they win 5% of the votes. By contrast, in Britain the first-past-the-post electoral system means that even third and fourth parties like the Liberals and Social Democrats win a far smaller proportion of seats in Parliament than of votes at elections. And in Britain it is virtually impossible in national elections, and very difficult in local elections, for new parties to get a foot in the door at all. Furthermore, while it may be true that all contemporary systems of politics and government reflect the factory mentality of the Industrial Age, the British two-party system today is more than usually retarded in this respect. Each of the two main parties, Conservative and Labour, still represents one side of the great divide between employers and employees, capital and labour, that was the basic structural feature of industrial society in the nineteenth century but is no longer the case today. The big question on the future of British politics in the last year or two has not been about how the new British party, corresponding to the German Greens, i.e. the Ecology Party,[1] will fare, but about whether an alliance between two existing groupings—the Liberals and ex-Labour Social Democrats—will be able to break the old two-party monopoly of political power.

On the other hand, perhaps because British people are not much excited by systematic thinking and intellectual ideas, any more in politics than in anything else, there has not been nearly so sharp a divide in Britain as in West Germany between those who are receptive to alternative or Green ideas and those who are not. Our pragmatism tends to blur boundaries. To take a comparatively trivial example, it is easy to find business executives in Britain who have a feel for the shift of values underlying the Green and alternative movements, and who are very ready to discuss its significance. More importantly, a tremendous number of associations, societies, lobbies, pressure groups and other organisations and groups of all kinds take an interest in every field that can be broadly defined as alternative or Green. They range from the explicitly political (including the Ecology Party and the environmental or ecology groups in the bigger parties), through

[1] [1997 note. The Ecology Party changed its name in 1985 and became the Green Party.]

parliamentary lobbies (such as the Parliamentary Liaison Group for Alternative Energy Strategies and the Green Alliance), campaigning organisations (such as the Campaign for Nuclear Disarmament, Greenpeace, and Friends of the Earth), professional and research associations (such as the Town and Country Planning Association and the Research Council for Complementary Medicine), to old established bodies (such as the Council for the Protection of Rural England and the Civic Trust). Their activities form a continuing spectrum from those of (conservative with a small 'c'), establishment bodies at one end to those of radical, marginal groups at the other.

A recent development in Britain, as in West Germany in the last few years, has been the forming of links between sections of the peace movement and the women's movement (e.g. the Greenham Common Women's Peace Camp), between sections of the peace movement and the Green movement (e.g. Green CND), and between sections of the women's movement and the Green movement (e.g. Women for Life on Earth). Many of those involved in these joint initiatives have radical socialist sympathies. Perhaps for that reason many other supporters of the peace movement, the Green movement, the women's movement, or—more generally—the alternative movement as a whole, tend to distance themselves from these particular forms of co-operation.

This underlines an important point. On the one hand, there is great scope for mutual support among different people and different groups now operating on different sectors of the new frontier. Through the Turning Point network I have myself been involved for some years in facilitating co-operation and mutual support of this kind.[2] On the other hand, it would be a serious mistake—at least for the time being—to suppose that these widely ranging groups should agree upon, or can be systematically co-ordinated in, a comprehensive strategy for social change and transformation. From time to time people do suggest this. They assume, as do the manifestos of conventional political parties, that no one can do anything together until they have first agreed about everything. What we have to understand now is that precisely the reverse of this is true: people can give one another a great deal of help and support in specific ways, and do not have to agree about everything else in order to do so.

So what are the prospects for Green politics in Britain? How should those who broadly share the concerns of the German Greens, and the view of the future which Fritjof Capra and Charlene Spretnak put forward in *Green*

[2] [1997 note. Alison Pritchard and I have been sending out a twice yearly *Turning Point* (latterly *Turning Point 2000*) newsletter since 1975, with the aim of spreading information and ideas about a people-centred, ecologically benign future.]

Politics, aim to proceed?

In the first place, the Ecology Party and the Green groups within the larger political parties are likely to grow in strength. Clearly, up to a point, they will be in competition with one another. Equally clearly, up to point, there will be scope for co-operation between them. For example, they will no doubt continue to hold joint meetings from time to time on topics of shared concern. Greens who want to be active in electoral politics will have to decide whether they are likely to be more effective in the Ecology Party or as members of a Green group within one of the larger parties. And at least some people who don't want to be politically active in the conventional sense will, nevertheless, want to keep good links with politically active Greens and to co-operate with them on specific projects from time to time.

However, political activity in the conventional sense is likely to play only one part among many in the growth of the Green or alternative movements in Britain in the next few years. In fact, I think we shall increasingly come to see that the politics of constructive social change can often be most effectively pursued outside the realm of conventional political activity. This may be particularly true in Britain where, as I have said, the existing system of politics and government is abnormally congested. In its most fundamental form, of course, the politics of change is about how we actually live our own lives, and about the effect we have on the people and the microstructures of society immediately around us on whom our way of living impinges directly. As the saying goes, 'Think globally, act locally'. But between lifestyle politics at one end of the spectrum and formal electoral politics at the other, there is an almost infinite number of ways in which we can positively help to create the new future we want.

It would be wrong to underestimate the importance of Green politics in the conventional sense. The political achievements of the German Greens have been an inspiration to very many people across the world. However, it is in the less formal, more open-ended, more pluralistic, more pervasive sense that I personally believe Green politics will become a really significant force for change in Britain in the next few years. Some Greens will agree with that, others may not. In either case, I warmly recommend *Green Politics* to British readers, as an invaluable source of information, encouragement and ideas.

Ironbridge, Shropshire
1984

7

Money

This is the text of a talk given in October 1987 in London at the Teilhard Centre for the Future of Man. Other aspects of money are discussed in Chapters 12 and 15.

I had been interested in the evolution of cultures since studying Greek and Roman history at Oxford. Arnold Toynbee's *A Study of History* and its account of the rise and fall of civilisations had fascinated me in the late 1940s. But I think it was Teilhard de Chardin's writings that first focused my attention on the evolution of consciousness—or the *noosphere*—as a key feature of human evolution. I can remember the excitement I felt as I read them when they came out in the late 1950s, starting with *The Phenomenon of Man*.

When I returned to Teilhard's thinking in the 1980s after my own ideas about the desirability of a SHE—as contrasted with a HE—future had crystallised, I realised that there were questions that needed to be asked. One of them, to do with the emergence of a global money system, is discussed here. But there were others too.

Four years later, in discussion following a paper of mine on 'Future Wealth and the Evolution of Consciousness'[1] at another Teilhard Conference in April 1991, I suggested that Teilhard's thinking had reflected the traditional Christian belief that humans should look up towards God and away from the rest of Creation beneath them. He saw human progress as an ascent from the material towards the etherial, in conflict with today's 'new paradigm' thinking, including 'creation-centred spirituality' which urges us not to try either to dominate or escape from Nature and our own corporeal bodies, but to enter into them fully as aspects of our true selves. He urged that:

> much greater resources—in money, men and organisation—[should be] employed in visiting and conquering the still unknown tracts of the world.[2]

In that passage and the pages immediately before it Teilhard—whose ideas, of course, took shape sixty or seventy years ago—appears to have supported a vision of progress not unlike what I have referred to as HE. This is, I believe, an aspect of Teilhard's thinking which today's Teilhardians should address.

January 1997

[1] Published in the *Teilhard Review*, Autumn 1991.
[2] *Human Energy*, Collins, 1969, pp. 133–4.

Money: I, Thou and It:

A Question Raised by the Emergence of a Global Money System

I am grateful for this opportunity to put before you for comment and criticism some thoughts that are still in the process of clarification. They are on an aspect of a topic which has occupied my attention for about twenty years now—the role of money in an evolving world society. On some aspects of that topic, I am conscious that my thinking has advanced during that time. But on others—including the emergence of a global money system as an aspect of what Teilhard de Chardin called the *noosphere*—I still have a problem, as you will see.

In the first part of what I have to say, I shall refer to Martin Buber's reflections, in '*I and Thou*',[3] on the personal, the interpersonal and the impersonal; and then to Teilhard's concept, in '*The Future of Man*'[4] of *noogenesis* as the evolution of a thinking web or envelope surrounding the earth, over and above the web of living matter that we call the biosphere.

Next, I shall discuss the growing role of money in the modern world, and suggest that it has tended to enlarge the province of the impersonal at the expense of the interpersonal. I shall then explain why we have to regard the emergence of a computerised, global money system as part of what Teilhard meant by the noosphere. This will leave us with the following question: Is noogenesis, as Teilhard supposed, a process of personalisation, or is it actually tending towards the enlargement of the impersonal?

Finally, I shall ask you to reflect on the personal, interpersonal and impersonal aspects of your own money relationships—all those incomings and outgoings of money to you and from you, which are part of the worldwide network of money links that connect each of us with other people and organisations. I shall mention a number of ways in which it may be possible to personalise these links, and I shall ask you to consider whether, and to what extent, these may be ways in which each one of us can help to personalise the noosphere.

---

[3] Martin Buber, *I And Thou*, 2nd edition, Scribners, New York, 1958, pp. 43–5 and 106.
[4] Pierre Teilhard de Chardin, *The Future of Man*, Collins, London, 1959.

I AND THOU AND THE FUTURE OF MAN

Martin Buber asserts—convincingly, it seems to me—that the development of the function of experiencing and using (i.e. treating people and things as 'It') comes about mostly through a decrease in the power to enter into relation (i.e. to treat them as 'Thou'). The province of It expands at the expense of the province of Thou. And, as he says, 'If a culture ceases to be centred in the living and continually renewed relational event, then it hardens into the world of It'.

Buber has a cautionary word for those of us who have been excited by recent market research and opinion surveys[5] suggesting that a shift is taking place from 'outer-directed' materialist and status values to 'inner-directed' values concerned with personal development and self-actualisation. He would have seen this as a shift from It-values to I-values, in accordance with his perception that man 'has divided his life into two tidily circled-off provinces, the province of It and the province of I. Institutions are "outside", where all sorts of aims are pursued…Feelings are "within", where life is lived and man recovers from institutions'.

As Buber puts it, those who are disillusioned with institutions say, 'Let the state be replaced by the community of love', and they imagine that this community will arise when people, out of free, abundant feeling, wish to live with one another. But, he says, this is not so. The true community does not arise through people having feelings for one another (though that is, indeed, necessary) but through people being in mutual living relation with one another.

Two brief points must now be made about Teilhard's concepts of noogenesis and the noosphere. The first point is that, in describing how progress, as the evolution of consciousness, has led to 'the growth, outside and above the biosphere, of an added planetary layer, an envelope of thinking substance', Teilhard made it clear that he saw noogenesis as a personalising process. He stressed that, if you accept the reality of noogenesis—the coming into being of the noosphere as an aspect of the evolution of consciousness— you are compelled to allow increasing room, in your vision of the future, for the value of personalisation 'because a Universe in process of psychic concentration is identical with a Universe that is acquiring a personality'. And he spoke of embracing 'a spirit of togetherness and personalising unification with all things'. The second point is to define what Teilhard was actually referring to when he spoke of the emergence of the noosphere. He makes it

---

[5] [1997 note. An accessible account of these is in Francis Kinsman, *Millennium: Towards Tomorrow's Society*, W. H. Allen, 1990.]

quite clear that he had in mind 'the extraordinary network of radio and television communications which...already link us all in a sort of etherised universal consciousness [and] the insidious growth of those astonishing electronic computers'.

While bearing the above two points in mind, it must also be noted that an important aspect of this emerging computerised, global telecommunications network is the emerging global system for transferring money and other financial claims electronically. And, as I shall suggest, there is, in fact, good reason to suppose that this and other developments in the use of money have tended towards the depersonalisation, not the personalisation, of our relationships—in other words, towards expanding the province of It and diminishing the province of Thou.

THE GROWING ROLE OF MONEY

The role of money in the lives of people and societies has grown immeasurably in the last few hundred years. Money plays the central role in late industrial society that religion played in the late Middle Ages. Then the local church was the most prominent building in most villages; today the prime sites in most high streets are occupied by branches of banks, building societies, and other financial concerns. The centres of medieval cities were dominated by cathedrals; today's city centres are dominated by the tower blocks of international banks. Today's army of accountants, bankers, tax-people, insurance brokers, stock jobbers, foreign exchange dealers and countless other specialists in money, is the modern counterpart of the medieval army of priests, friars, monks, nuns, abbots and abbesses, pardoners, summoners and other specialists in religious procedures and practices. The theologians of the late Middle Ages have their counterpart in the economists of the industrial age. Then they argued about how many angels could stand on the point of a pin; now they argue about how the money supply should be measured. Financial mumbo-jumbo holds us in thrall today, as religious mumbo-jumbo held our ancestors then.

Whereas in pre-industrial times most people, living in rural village communities, provided most of the necessities of life for themselves and one another directly through their own work, most people in modern society are almost wholly dependent on money for the goods and services they need—either to purchase them themselves or to be provided with them by public services paid for with public money.

As the role of money has become greater in the lives of people and society, the institutions set up to handle money have become bigger and more remote. In step with increasing centralisation in industry and government, financial institutions have become more centralised. Small local banks have been taken over by bigger banks and turned into local branches of national banking networks. Only in very exceptional cases are local financial institutions found today with the function of channelling local money into investment in local enterprises and projects.

The investment of money, then, has become less personal and less local, as has the spending of money in supermarkets instead of local corner shops, and the earning of money from faceless employing organisations instead from personal employers. As increasing numbers of people have acquired savings to invest—in pensions for their retirement and in mortgages for their houses, as well as in other forms of saving—they have not been expected to take a personal interest in how those savings are used. Just as employees have become content to hand over responsibility to employing organisations to direct the purposes of their work, so savers have been content to hand over responsibility to a bank, or a pension fund, or a building society, or some other financial institution, to decide what use is to be made of their money.

With this has come a growing tendency to try to make money out of money rather than out of useful activity. This has resulted in the huge growth of stock markets, money markets, bond markets, currency markets and other financial markets throughout the world, and in the ever-growing demand for capital assets like land and property, not mainly to make good use of them but in the hope of selling them later at a capital gain. And this in turn has been one of the contributing factors to the massive expansion of borrowing and debt—personal, corporate, national and international—that has taken place in the last thirty or forty years.

As the use of money and our attitudes to money have become more impersonal in these ways, money itself has become more abstract and less material. Not many generations ago most of the money in common use was of metal, and most money transactions involved the handing of metal from one person to another. Since then, money has evolved into paper (e.g. bank notes and cheques) and is now taking the form of electronic information in the interconnected computer systems of banks and other large organisations. A computerised global communications network has developed, through which money transactions are carried out by crediting and debiting the accounts of the parties to the transaction. The whole process is a much less personal way of making payments than the person-to-person transfer of coin and paper.

The upshot of all this is that we now have a world money system, which has clearly developed into one aspect of Teilhard's noosphere. In this system, the money markets and stock markets of Tokyo, London and New York are linked in a continually active web of financial transactions twenty-four hours a day. Many of these transactions are activated automatically by computers programmed to buy and sell currencies and bonds, stocks, and shares, when their price level reaches a certain point. The people operating the system and carrying out the transactions know nothing and care nothing about the lives of the people ultimately affected by these financial transactions. Their work has become depersonalised to a degree which fully justifies Buber's question: 'Can the servant of Mammon say Thou to his money?'.

MONEY AS AN ASPECT OF THE SCIENTIFIC WORLDVIEW

Money is a quantitative calculus of value, providing a measure of the value of the work we do and the things we exchange with one another. The growth of money in people's lives and in the life of societies has represented a shift out of what is known as the informal economy, in which people provide goods and services for themselves and one another directly, into the formal economy in which people produce goods and provide services for monetary exchange. Exchange values now predominate over use values.

This shift has been part of the larger shift that has taken place in recent centuries in favour of what can be quantified. It has been paralleled, for example, by the growing importance of clock time and calendar time, as contrasted with the daily, monthly and annual rhythms set by the sun, moon and seasons. More generally, it has been paralleled by the growth of science and technology and measurement in every sphere. This shift in favour of the quantitative can be traced back to the dualism established by Descartes between matter (*res extensa*) and mind (*res cogitans*). It is epitomised in Lord Kelvin's famous dictum:

> When you can measure what you are speaking of and express it in numbers, you know that on which you are discoursing, but when you cannot measure it and express it in number, your knowledge is of a very meagre and unsatisfactory kind.

The effect of this shift, of which the expanded role of money is one aspect, has been to exalt the province of It at the expense of the provinces of I and—particularly—Thou. In the last few hundred years we have distanced ourselves from nature and the universe, which we have come to regard as a machine, to be explained from outside by natural scientists, and to be manipulated from outside by engineers, industrialists and factory farmers. Similarly, we have distanced ourselves from other people and society. We have learned to think of people as impersonal role-players—consumers, employees, pensioners, and so on—cogs in the society machine. And we have come to suppose that people and society can be understood and manipulated from outside as if they are things—by economists, market-researchers, politicians, advertisers, and so on.

The depersonalising effects of developments in the sphere of money can thus be seen as part of a larger evolutionary trend—in conflict with Teilhard's idea of personalising noogenesis. Whether one regards money as a device for institutionalising trust or, as some think, for institutionalising mistrust, either way it seems to have been an increasingly powerful force for expanding the province of It.

PERSONALISING THE USE OF MONEY

At this point, then, let us take a personal approach. Let us think about the incomings and outgoings of money to and from ourselves. Each one of us receives inward payments from other people and organisations—as wages, salaries or fees for work, as pensions and social security benefits, as dividends and interest on our savings, as gifts and prizes, or from the sale of property and possessions, from realising savings, and so on. Each one of us makes outward payments for such things as food, clothing, household expenses, transport, holidays and leisure, mortgage payments, insurance premiums, taxes, and so on. All these inward and outward payments link us into the network of money transactions that flow through our society and the world. Each of us is a nodal point on that global network. Participation in that network is one of the things that binds us into the larger system of society, and the pattern taken by these flows of money to us and from us helps to determine the nature of that larger system.

Although we have been increasingly conditioned to regard most of these inward and outward flows of money to and from ourselves impersonally and amorally, the fact is that each of us does have a degree of choice over their size and direction. If we disapprove of certain types of work or certain types of people, we can decide against earning money from them, and we can exercise the same kind of control over our spending and saving decisions. In other words, each of us has some scope to determine how our money transactions affect society and the world, and to exercise conscious, personal care in this respect.

If this scope is to be enlarged, three things will be necessary. The first is a growing awareness that we do have this power of conscious choice and that, by exercising it, we can help to influence the kind of society and the kind of world we live in—awareness that this exercise of power as earners, spenders and savers is one of the principal ways in which we can personally help to shape the further evolution of society and the world. Second, in addition to growing awareness, people will need to acquire the knowledge and skills to enable them to direct their earning and spending in ways that are for the better—knowledge, for example, of how the money they spend or invest will be used by its recipients, and the skills needed to change existing spending and investing patterns for the better. Third, the institutions of society, such as banks, supermarkets and so on, which loom large in our money relationships, will have to be persuaded to respect our wish to handle these relationships more consciously; they will have to learn to help us to do so.

There are, in fact, signs that moves towards more conscious earning, consuming and investing are under way. Although recent high levels of unemployment in all the industrialised countries have brought pressure on many people to accept jobs which they find distasteful, they have also provided the occasion for increasing numbers of people to earn their living in self-employment or community enterprises or other forms of what I have called 'ownwork'—that is, work which people themselves regard as valuable.[6] A 'conscious consumer' movement is growing, partly in the form of boycotting purchases from what are seen as undesirable sources,[7] partly in the form of positive discrimination in favour of certain products (e.g. 'green' products), and partly in the form of reducing unnecessary consumption (e.g. as recommended by the Lifestyle Movement[8]). So far as saving and investment are concerned, there is a strongly growing movement for 'ethical' or 'social' investment—again, partly in the negative sense of enabling people to avoid investing their savings in things they disapprove of (e.g. tobacco or armaments), and partly in the more positive sense of enabling people to channel their savings into enterprises and projects which they themselves wish to support.

CONCLUSION

If millions of people over the coming years were to begin to develop these kinds of conscious controls over their own patterns of money inflows and outflows, that could have an important personalising effect on the further

[6] For a fuller discussion see James Robertson, *Future Work*, Gower/Temple Smith, 1985.

[7] [1997 note. In the original 1987 paper, I gave South Africa as an example of a source of goods which conscious consumers boycotted. How things have changed! I recently saw South African firms (with good employment policies for black employees) listed among the kinds of firms which ethical investors should positively favour.]

[8] The Lifestyle Movement's members undertake to live simply 'so that others may simply live'.

evolution of the noosphere. However, it is hard to see how far that could go, and we are left, with difficult questions.

One result of the development of the noosphere, including the emerging global money system, is that each of us today can be directly connected with, and can transact with, many more people all over the world than our ancestors could. With how many people is it possible to be in living mutual relation—to have an I-Thou relationship? Could it ever be possible for several billion people to enjoy I-Thou relationships with one another? What would that be like? How might the money system support such relationships, and how would we have to reform it to enable it to do so?

Cholsey, Oxfordshire
October 1987

8

Towards a Post-Modern Worldview

In the late 1980s and early 1990s I took part in several conferences in Dublin at the invitation of Father Sean Healy and Sister Brigid Reynolds of what is now the Justice Commission of the Conference of Religious of Ireland. For many years they have been publishing outstandingly constructive proposals for rectifying economic and social injustices, both in Ireland and in the wider world economy.

On one of these occasions they introduced me to John Quinn of Irish Radio RTE. He subsequently arranged for me to give the 1990 Open Mind Guest Lecture. This was broadcast in Dublin on RTE on l0th October 1990, under the heading 'Health, Wealth and Wisdom for the 21st Century: The Missing Ethical Dimension in Science, Economics and Lifestyles'. This chapter is the text of that lecture.

On this same visit to Dublin John Quinn recorded six half-hour interviews with me on *The Sane Alternative*, and these were later broadcast by RTE in weekly instalments.

January 1997

Towards a Post-Modern Worldview

I wonder what 1992 means for you?

For most businesspeople, bureaucrats and politicians in the countries of Western Europe like yours and mine, 1992 means the European single market. I hesitate to call this a short-sighted and narrow view, taken by those who cannot see further than the end of their nose or—as the Indian saying has it— wider than the tips of their ears. But the historical significance of 1992 is much more far-reaching, much less parochial, than the European single market. In 1992, for the first time in history, representatives of all the peoples of the world will come together to discuss our common future—at the United Nations Conference on Environment and Development in Brazil. This will be held on the 20th anniversary of the 1972 Stockholm conference on the environment. It will be the first major landmark in the follow-up to the Brundtland Commission's report *Our Common Future*, published in 1987. And, more significant still, 1992 will be the 500th anniversary of Columbus's landing in the Western hemisphere.

Many people of European, or Western, outlook will celebrate Columbus's achievement as the 'discovery' of America—as if the indigenous peoples of the continent did not exist and were of no account. From that Eurocentric point of view, 12th October 1492 was an unqualified 'good thing'—in Sellar's and Yeatman's phrase from *1066 And All That*[1]—a historic milestone in the upward progress of the human race from savagery to civilisation.

To the indigenous peoples of North and South America it is a different story. They will have little to celebrate in 1992. To them, Columbus's discovery was a historic disaster—leading to the loss of their traditional freedoms and livelihoods, the devastation of their lands, and the destruction of their cultures. That story continues today, for those like the Yanomani and other forest peoples of the Amazon basin. And not only for them. The same is true for other non-European peoples all over the planet. For them Columbus's discovery in 1492, and Vasco da Gama's sailing to India in 1498, signify the beginning of half a millennium of European world domination—at first Christian and latterly secular.

[1] W. C. Sellar and R. J. Yeatman, *1066 And All That*, Magnet, 1930c., repr. 1984.

I don't want to deny that this 500-year epoch has brought progress of many kinds—though this raises questions about how we define progress. A generation or two ago, it might have made sense to interpret the competitive success of European, or Western, culture simply as an example of social Darwinism—the survival of the fittest. But, as things are now turning out, that has become a sick joke. For it is the kinds of progress European culture has brought to the world, and the direction of further development it entails, that are now the gravest threat to human survival.

Weapons development is one obvious aspect of this. But more deeply dangerous, because a little less obvious, is the vision of the good life—the high consumption lifestyle—which we relentlessly promote worldwide as the main goal of development. I'm not just thinking of African villagers watching Dallas on TV, though that is an example. With the 5 billion people now in the world, we are already threatening the Earth's life support systems. Projections show that the number will ultimately rise to 10 or 15 billion. If development, as we now promote it, were fully successful and all these 10 or 15 billion people were to consume as many resources and cause as much pollution as today's rich minority (which includes you and me), today's ecological impacts would be multiplied 20 or 30 times. Anyone who thinks this makes sense must be crazy. I said that the dangers might not be immediately obvious. But, in fact, even some mainstream economists are now beginning to put out blueprints for a greener economy.

We urgently need to switch to a new development path. We need a new way of economic life and thought. It must be enabling for people, not disabling and dependency-creating, as much economic progress is today. And it must be conserving for the Earth, not ecologically damaging and destructive. This switch to a new economics must be part of a larger 'paradigm shift'. Conventional economics is part of our prevailing worldview. That worldview—and the existing world order based on it—are beginning to break down. One of the main tasks—the historic role, you might say—for us who are living at this time, is to help to bring into being a new worldview and a new world order. This has tremendous implications, and there are very many aspects we could explore. What I want to do in this talk is to look at the need for a new economics in the context of that larger paradigm shift—and that means in the context of the history and the future of ideas.

THE EUROPEAN INHERITANCE

The addictive, destructive and unsustainable approach to economic life which now prevails in almost every corner of the world is linked to the dominance of European culture and the Western worldview. So where did we Europeans go wrong? Where did our European inheritance play us false? One view is that the damage was done when the medieval order in Europe broke down. Although we can't go back to the Middle Ages, looking at what happened then may help us to see our way forward now.

The medieval worldview was hierarchical, static, religious, and moral. The medieval hierarchy started with God in his Heaven at the top, followed by archangels and angels. Then came humankind, below the angels but above the beasts. Highest among humans were popes and kings, followed by princes and bishops and nobles, and so on down the line to the poorest of the common people. Then came the animal kingdom, with the vegetable and mineral orders of creation following on below. The medieval picture of the world was static. Evolution played no part in it. People were expected to remain in the station in which God had placed them in society—the rich man in his castle and the poor man at his gate. Sons would follow in their fathers' footsteps. The village baker's son would become the village baker after him, the miller's son the miller, and so on. There was not much scope for yuppies in the Middle Ages. Upward mobility—and downward mobility, for that matter—were exceptions to the rule. Above all, the medieval worldview was religious and moral. The central purpose of human life—the purpose that gave it meaning—was to save one's soul for eternal life with God and his angels in another world from this one. The workings of God's creation, including the behaviour of human beings, were governed by God's laws. Economic transactions and relationships were subject to moral law: the just price and the just wage were part of the divinely sanctioned web of rights and obligations that held everyone and everything together.

This hierarchical, static, religious and moral worldview, which had been dominant in the middle ages, broke down about 500 years ago, as did the structures of society and ways of life based on it. It broke down because the old order had become unsustainable, and because the way to a new future was being opened up by pioneers like Christopher Columbus (1451–1506) and Niccolò Machiavelli (1469–1527) and Copernicus (1473–1543), breaking through previous limitations of territory, behaviour and thought.

The same dynamic—breakdown of the old and breakthrough to the new—is at work today. The worldview now dominant, and the structures of society and the ways of life based on it, are becoming unsustainable. And pioneers in many fields—including the growing worldwide movement for a new economics—are opening up the way to a new future, whose characteristic worldview, structures of society and ways of life we still have to crystallise.

ORIGINS OF THE MODERN WORLDVIEW

When the medieval worldview broke down, it took some time—nearly 300 years—for the modern worldview to crystallise in its place. This time, the process will have to be quicker. Nonetheless, what happened then is interesting and relevant for us today.

Among the thinkers who helped to shape the modern worldview were René Descartes (1596–1650), Francis Bacon (1561–1626), Isaac Newton (1642–1727) and Thomas Hobbes (1588–1679). Theirs were among the ideas that Adam Smith (1723–1790) took up when, in the Enlightenment of the 18th century, he systematised the modern approach to economic life and thought.

Descartes divided reality into two categories, *res cogitans* and *res extensa* (thinking matter and extended matter). In due course, knowledge and science concentrated on, and came to regard as real, only the second part of that Cartesian duality—that is, those aspects of human experience and understanding which are material and measurable and outside ourselves. Descartes' analytical method encouraged us to split those aspects of reality up into separate fields so that now, for example, our conventional way of understanding what we take to be health, wealth, and wisdom is splintered among different professional disciplines called medicine, economics and philosophy.

Bacon encouraged knowledge and science to focus on harnessing and exploiting the resources of Nature—Nature corresponding more or less to Descartes' *res extensa*. Bacon taught us to torture Nature in order to learn her secrets, and to use her for, as he put it, 'the relief of the inconveniences of man's estate', and now we are beginning to inflict catastrophic damage on the natural world.

Newton's example led science to interpret reality in the form of mechanistic, mathematically structured, value-free systems, and scientists now teach us to understand the workings of the universe in terms of numbers, and to assume that neither it nor any of its component parts are guided by purposes or moral choices.

What most people probably remember about Hobbes is his argument that since —regardless of what theory might say—moral or divine law does not in fact effectively control people's behaviour, they must submit to control by an earthly sovereign. Otherwise their lives are bound to be 'poor, solitary, nasty, brutish and short'. Hobbes' significance for us is that, like Machiavelli before him, he taught his successors to see human society not as it ought to be, but as it actually appeared to be—a competitive struggle for power; and very many people now take it for granted that success in life means getting one up on other people—or at least keeping up with the Jones's.

It was on ideas such as these, then, that Adam Smith drew in systematising his—and our—understanding of economic life. They are all ideas that we now need to question. For example, Smith followed Descartes in excluding from economic understanding the less tangible aspects of human experience and activity, such as those we now call 'participation', 'self-fulfilment' and 'self-development'. He followed Bacon in accepting that economic life was about exploiting the resources of Nature for human advancement. He followed Hobbes in interpreting economic life as a competitive struggle for power—in particular, power over the use and the products of other people's labour. He followed Newton in seeing economic life as a value-free system, governed by its own impersonal laws. Smith's 'invisible hand' of supply and demand meant that God no longer had a part to play in economic life. It made God redundant—put Him out of a job. And the consequences of Smith's ideas was to exclude not just religion from economics, but morality too. He taught that the economic system operates in the best interest of all if each pursues his own self-interest. As he put it, 'It is not from the benevolence of the butcher, the brewer or the baker that we expect our dinner, but from their regard to their own interest.'

Another important point that Smith took for granted was that economic life revolves around money—prices, wages, profits, rents, and so forth. Now, money means numbers; and there's a very significant parallel between the emphasis on numerical data in modern science and the emphasis on money values in modern economic life.

The supremacy of quantitative values in modern scientific knowledge was nicely put by Lord Kelvin:

> When you can measure what you are speaking of and express it in numbers, you know that on which you are discoursing, but when you cannot measure it and express it in numbers, your knowledge is of a very meagre and unsatisfactory kind.[2]

As with knowledge, so with value. Money puts numbers on value, and conventional economic understanding regards as very meagre and unsatisfactory the value of goods, services, and work (such as what used to be called women's work), which are not paid for with money. In fact, so far as economists are concerned, if you can't count something, it doesn't count. They just don't notice it. They blank it out.

This has led some critics—half-humorously—to interpret economics as a form of brain damage. Others, in similar vein, think economists are suffering from a lack of investment in up-to-date capital equipment. But I

---

[2] [1997 note. This quotation was also included in Chapter 7.]

mustn't start telling jokes about economists or we'll be here all night. The serious point is that there is an aspect of reality here which we are going to have to rethink in the post-modern world.

We are going to have to learn to value other forms of knowledge—personal, intuitive, moral and spiritual—as well as the knowledge offered by conventional science. We are going to have to learn to value what are called alternative or complementary approaches to health, as well as conventional medicine. We are going to have to learn to value informal economic activities—everything people do for themselves and one another without either paying or being paid—as well as activities whose value can be measured in money.

It will not be easy to marry the qualitative and the quantitative. They often conflict. For example, scientifically controlled monitoring of mystical experiences may destroy the conditions in which mystical experiences take place—like looking for darkness with a torch. But we are going to have to find ways to systematise new understandings—new theories—about knowledge, health and wealth which give full weight to both qualitative and quantitative values. Perhaps future historians of thought will see these new understandings and theories as post-scientific and post-medical and post-economic.

RECOVERY OF PURPOSE

So let us now compare the modern worldview with the medieval worldview.

The modern worldview has remained hierarchical; it continues to see the world in terms of ladders. But it is mobile, not static. It sees human progress in terms of climbing a ladder of knowledge and power. It sees human life as a competition to climb higher than other people up ladders of career and status and wealth and power. And, when it can, it judges progress in terms of numerical measurements. But, most importantly, the modern worldview has excluded religion and morality. It has offered no meaning to human life, no goal at the top of the ladders, no purpose in climbing the ladders other than climbing for its own sake. 'Ladders To Nowhere'—that is the name of the game the modern worldview asks us to play.

Even the most advanced scientists still suspect the very idea of purpose, and assume that what they call 'objectivity' excludes it. In his recent book *The Ages Of Gaia*[3] James Lovelock endorses the view that 'the cornerstone of scientific method is the postulate that Nature is objective. True knowledge can

[3] James Lovelock, *The Ages of Gaia*, Oxford University Press, 1988, p. 214.

never be gained by attributing "purpose" to phenomena.' That's what Lovelock says, and many people have hailed his Gaia theory as a new milestone in science. But can you really understand people without attributing purposes to them? Or cats? Or earthworms? Or plants? Or the component parts of any organism? And who is to say—how could anyone know?—that true knowledge can be gained of the Universe itself by assuming in advance that it has no purpose?

These are difficult questions. But one thing is absolutely clear. The theoretical notion that scientific knowledge and economic behaviour are value-free has left a vacuum. And in practice this vacuum has been filled by values of power and greed and competition.

In short, our European worldview has led us—and now the rest of the world—to err and stray from the ways of wisdom. There is now no health in us, in the old senses of wholeness and holiness. And the kind of wealth we strive for is often not wealth in the old sense of well-being—whether the well-being of other people, or of the Earth, or even of ourselves. The world's crisis today is a crisis of values.

REVIVAL OF ETHICAL VALUES

We have seen that the breakdown of the medieval worldview meant the decline of an existing moral order and the rise of a new scientific order. By contrast, I see the breakdown of the modern worldview as the decline of the existing scientific order and the rise of a new moral order. This will be clearer to future historians than it is to us now, but the signs are already there.

Take economics. The existing science of economics has told us that the chief aim of economic life is to make money values grow. So a national economy's chief aim has been money-measured economic growth, a business's chief aim has been financial profit, and the chief aim of consumers and investors has been to get best value for money from their purchases and the best financial return from their investments. But in the 1980s these assumptions have begun to be questioned—even in the most respectable quarters.

For example, the World Bank and the International Monetary Fund are now beginning to recognise the devastating consequences of conventional economic orthodoxy for many Third World countries, and are beginning to face up to the need to resolve the long-running Third World debt crisis. Meanwhile, many people all round the world are not just feeling that the systematic transfer of wealth from poorer and less powerful peoples to richer and more powerful ones is wrong—which it clearly is. They are also recognising it as an inevitable outcome of a competitive, amoral economic system, driven by the aim of making money values grow and regulated by the impersonal mechanics of supply and demand.

Another example is from the Brundtland Commission's report, *Our Common Future*. Brundtland pointed out that environmental policy and economic policy must be integrated. It is no longer good enough for environmental policy just to clear up the messes left by economic development, and to deal with what Brundtland called 'after-the-fact repair of damage: reforestation, reclaiming desert lands, rebuilding urban environments, restoring natural habitats, and rehabilitating wild lands'. And it is no longer good enough for economic policy just to 'create wealth' in the narrow and abstract conventional sense, regardless of the environment.

In almost exactly the same way, the World Health Organisation, with its strategy on Health For All by the Year 2000, has begun to shift the emphasis away from remedial sickness services to the positive creation of healthier conditions of life. And WHO's conclusion on health, like Brundtland's on the environment, is that health goals must be brought into economic policy. Again, 'creating wealth' in the conventional sense is seen as too abstract and too narrow. Economic policy must pursue real purposes, like maintaining a good environment and enabling people to be healthy, and not just money-measured growth.

It is not just the conventional goals of economic policy that are beginning to be rethought, but also the conventional ways of measuring economic progress. A lot of work is getting under way—in the United Nations and national governments, as well as in activist groups like the New Economics Foundation—to develop and introduce new economic indicators and targets. This involves trying to improve existing money-measured indicators like the Gross National Product (GNP). But, more importantly, it also involves supplementing these money-measured abstractions—perhaps eventually replacing them—by bringing indicators of the state of the real world—such as people's health or the quality of the air and water and so on—to bear upon economic decision making.

There is a parallel at the personal level to bringing real goals and purposes, and not just conventional money-measured criteria, into economic policy-making. I am talking about the increasing numbers of consumers and investors who are trying to be 'green', or 'ethical', or 'socially responsible'. They are deciding to bring their values into their economic lives, and to use their purchasing power and their investing power to support the kinds of projects and causes which they themselves favour. They are rejecting the conventional idea that their only economic goal should be to get the best money value for themselves.

Even in science itself the idea of value-free objectivity is increasingly under fire. It is becoming more widely understood that, in many fields, objective knowledge is not even a theoretical possibility because the observer cannot observe the subject matter without affecting its behaviour in one way or another. In that respect the particle physicist is in the same boat as the anthropologist studying a tribal society.

There is also growing awareness that the idea of value-free objectivity in science, just as in economics, has been used as a smokescreen by powerful groups—governments, business, finance, the military and the professions, including the scientific establishment itself—to use science in their own interests. In recent years more and more people have become concerned about the purposes for which science is used.

EVOLVING A NEW WORLDVIEW

Those few examples of ethical purposes and moral choices being brought back into areas of practice and thought which the modern worldview has seen as value-free are pointers to the new worldview of the future. But what are they pointing us to? I can only give you my own personal thoughts. They are not pointing back to the Middle Ages. Even if we could go back, the medieval picture of a static world is at odds with our knowledge of evolution today. The medieval assumption that the Christian God is superior to the divinities of other faiths does not fit the emerging multicultural one-world community of today. The medieval beliefs that God is masculine, that men are superior to women, and that humans are superior to Nature—special creatures with special kinds of souls to whom God has given dominion over the rest of His creation—clash with the feminist and ecological understandings of today.

Perhaps, then, in this coming post-European era of world history, we should turn to non-European faiths like Buddhism or Hinduism, or to the cultures of peoples like the North American Indians? They all offer wisdom concerning human life and the place of human beings in the world—insights that have been lost in modern European culture. But, like Christianity, they have been quite unable to halt the worldwide juggernaut of conventional, secular, consumerist development, although it runs altogether contrary to their teachings. I am sure their insights will be reflected in the new worldview that eventually emerges. But, stemming as they did from small agricultural and pastoral and hunter-gatherer societies of long ago, we cannot realistically expect them to offer us a new post-modern worldview more or less ready-made off the peg. No. We should draw on the wisdom and insights of the past. But the peoples of the world today and tomorrow will have to create the new worldview afresh out of our own lives and predicaments, out of our own contemporary experience and understanding.

I think the new worldview will be a developmental worldview, in which purpose is combined with evolution in a new vision of progress. I think it will comprehend person and society, planet and universe, as aspects of the evolutionary process—a process that includes the evolution of consciousness and purpose—and perhaps of divinity too. I think that what gives value and meaning to our lives will be the part we play in this process: developing our own potential, enabling other people to do the same, contributing to the development of our society and the emerging one-world human community, maintaining and perhaps even enhancing the natural riches of our planet, and consciously participating in the evolution of the cosmos.

This is the wider context in which the idea of a new, enabling and conserving, economics makes sense to me. It is in this context, I foresee, that people in the next century and the next millennium will seek health, wealth and wisdom. It is in this context that we should interpret current issues—such as closer co-operation in Western Europe, or the collapse of communism in Eastern Europe, or the crisis in the Middle East. And it is in this context, I believe, that we should now be preparing to chart our common future in 1992.

Cholsey, Oxfordshire
1990

9

Health

This chapter was published in Sara Parkin (ed.), *Green Light on Europe*, Heretic Books, London, 1991.

Lengthier papers on health, arising from collaborations with Ilona Kickbusch and her colleagues at the World Health Organisation's Regional Office for Europe in Copenhagen, had included:

- *Health, Wealth and the New Economics: an Agenda for a Healthier World*, based on papers and discussions at the 1985 meeting of The Other Economic Summit (TOES), and
- *Scenarios for Lifestyles and Health*, published in European Monographs in Health Education Research, Issue 6, Scottish Health Education Group, 1984.

When I presented the latter at a seminar for WHO European Region chief medical officers in Corfu in September 1985, the Soviet bloc CMOs unanimously protested that it was unnecessary, indeed insulting, to ask them to discuss scenarios (alternative futures) for lifestyles and health, since their plans were already firmly in place to achieve Health for All by the Year 2000! A happier memory is of helping to draft the Ottawa Charter at WHO's first International Conference on Health Promotion in 1986.

January 1997

New Commonhealth

No, it's not a misprint. I believe that commonhealth will be one of the energising ideas of the 21st century. In twenty or thirty years' time, it will seem no stranger than commonwealth does today. Indeed, the two ideas will reinforce one another, as new insights spread about health and wealth and the links of both with ecological sustainability.

That is what this chapter is about. It weaves together strands that a mechanistic culture has dealt with separately. The first section is about the movement for a new public health, which emphasises health, rather than sickness. The second is about the movement for a new economics, which emphasises wealth as well-being. The third is about the need to integrate these new approaches to health and wealth with one another, and with a new approach to natural ecosystems—a vital aspect of the post-Brundtland '1992 Process'. The concluding section discusses the particular significance of all this for Europe.

HEALTH, NOT SICKNESS

One aspect of the modern secular culture which stemmed originally from Europe but now dominates the whole world, is that we pay more attention to sickness than to health. Health workers and others in the health business have been able to make a better living out of sick people than out of healthy people, and politicians have found more votes in sickness than in health; so much so that the word 'health' is now used more often than not to mean sickness. Our health services, health professionals, health statistics, health policies and health insurance, for example, are primarily sickness services, etc. Our Health Department is a sickness department, and our Health Ministers are sickness ministers.

This modern tendency to treat health from a remedial point of view, after the event, has been paralleled by our approach to the environment. As the Brundtland World Commission on Environment and Development reported:[1]

[1] *Our Common Future*, Oxford University Press, 1987 p. 39.

environmental management practices have focused largely upon after-the-fact repair of damage: reforestation, reclaiming desert lands, rebuilding urban environments, restoring natural habitats, and rehabilitating wild lands.

In just the same way, health policies and health services have concentrated on remedying sickness once it has occurred rather than on positively promoting healthy conditions of life and enabling people to be healthier. Economic policies have reinforced this remedial approach. Far from aiming to improve health and the environment, they have treated health and environmental risks and damage as unfortunate but inevitable side effects of economic progress, to be minimised and then remedied—if possible—after the event.

That is one way in which the idea of commonhealth cuts across today's conventional approach to health. Another is that it recognises health as something more than an individual condition. Conventional health services have concentrated on the provision of care to individuals. Conventional health education and health promotion have been mainly designed to encourage individuals to look after their own health—an approach that all too easily degenerates into 'blaming the victim', when ill-health is due to social and environmental circumstances outside people's control. Community medicine and public health have come low in the pecking order of the medical and health professions. Commonhealth, by contrast, emphasises our common interest in creating and maintaining conditions that will enable us to live healthy lives. Such conditions include physical, social, political and economic environments that make 'the healthier choice the easier choice'—for politicians, public officials and businesspeople, as well as for people in their personal and family lives.

Another point of difference between the idea of commonhealth and the conventional approach to health is the emphasis conventionally placed on new drugs, new equipments and other new medical technologies. The conventional assumption is that advances in health—and in all other fields—are to be achieved primarily through scientific research and the development of improved technology. The commonhealth approach does not dispute the importance of technology, any more than the concept of commonwealth disputes it. But it emphasises that the key to health creation, like the key to genuine wealth creation, lies in the social and environmental factors which determine how technology is actually developed and used.

It would be wrong to think that commonhealth is just a pie-in-the-sky idea. Since the early 1980s the European Regional Office of the World Health Organisation (WHO–Europe) has been alerting us to the need for a new understanding of health and a new approach to health policy. The 1982 publication, *Health Crisis 2000*,[2] based on the WHO European Regional

[2] Peter O' Neil, *Health Crisis 2000*, Heinemann, 1982.

Strategy for Attaining Health for All by the Year 2000, warned that:

> there could be a health crisis by the year 2000 unless radical steps are taken by the public, the professions, industry, and the governments of the Region. This is no idle warning. A careful analysis of trends in health and disease, made over the past three years by representatives of the medical profession and the health ministries of the Region's 33 Member States, has produced ominous signs that our health policies since the Second World War have set us on a dangerous course. The glittering attraction of high technology and the public's demand for 'miracle cures' have meant that we have almost abandoned the principle of self-care in a 'caring community'. Instead of promoting health and preventing disease, we have invested the bulk of our health budgets in 'disease palaces' which have really only cured our acute illnesses.

Through the 1980s WHO–Europe has taken the lead in WHO's work on lifestyles and health, health promotion, health education, healthy cities and healthy public policies. Key milestones have included: the Ottawa Charter for Health Promotion, issued at the first International Conference on Health Promotion in 1986; the launch of the Healthy Cities project in 1986; the second International Conference on Health Promotion in Adelaide in 1988, which concentrated on healthy public policies; and the European Charter on Environment and Health, issued in 1989. A third International Conference, to be held in Sundsvall, Sweden, in June 1991, will focus on creating supportive environments for health.

The impact of these efforts on actual developments may have been disappointing so far, but the ideas behind them have laid the foundations for rapid progress when the breakthrough comes. They are briefly summarised below.

The Ottawa Charter affirmed the importance of fundamental living conditions and resources, including a stable ecosystem, as prerequisites for health. It defined health promotion as the process of enabling people to take control over and improve their health, and stressed the importance of community empowerment. It outlined a comprehensive strategy for health promotion based on healthy public policies, supportive environments, community action, the development of personal skills, and a reorientation of health services. It pointed towards a new approach to public health in keeping with late 20th century needs.

The Healthy Cities project in Europe covers 30 cities in 19 countries, committed to achieving greater support for healthy local policies from political decision-makers and local communities. The spread of the healthy cities idea has, in fact gone, much wider than the cities directly participating in the project. A total of some 300 are now involved.

The Adelaide recommendations stressed that healthy public policy must involve all sectors of government decision-making, including especially those not specifically responsible for 'health'. Public policy in such fields as agriculture, education, social welfare, housing, transport and economics, should ensure that everyone has equitable access to the prerequisites for health. New systems of political accountability should make policy-makers answer for the health impacts of their policies.

The European Charter on Environment and Health was issued in December 1989 by the Ministers of Environment and of Health from the European Region of WHO, meeting together for the first time. The Charter lays down entitlements and responsibilities for a healthy environment, principles for public policy, and priorities. It has been endorsed by the European Commission as a guideline for future action by the Community. Its Principle 6, that 'the health of individuals and communities should take clear precedence over considerations of economy and trade', has been ignored so far in the process of creating a European single market—as indeed have environmental considerations. The Charter must be brought to bear on further economic integration in Europe up to and beyond 1992.

WEALTH AS WELL-BEING[3]

So far as health is concerned, conventional economic policies have had many damaging effects. For example, conventional economic growth involves treating as additions to well-being such things as the expansion of the tobacco industry and the arms trade, investments in unhealthy processes, and the advertising of unhealthy products and lifestyles. In industrialised countries, conventional economic development fails to solve the problems of poverty and deprivation that lead to ill-health. In Third World countries, it positively creates health problems—for example by depriving peasant peoples of their traditional livelihoods. All over the world, conventional development has created widespread health problems associated with various forms of chemical and other pollution.

Underlying the health-damaging effects of conventional economic practice is the assumption that the creation of wealth and the creation of health have nothing to do with each other. Effort expended on safeguarding or improving health is actually regarded as a cost—as a drag and a constraint on economic and business growth. A new understanding of wealth creation is

[3] [1997 note. In *Green Light on Europe* this chapter included at this point a short description of conventional economics, new economics, and the new economics movement. This is omitted here to avoid duplication with previous chapters. The relevance to health of a new approach to economics was then developed as follows.]

needed. Health creation must be seen as an aspect of it, and investment in health must be recognised as an economically valuable form of investment.

This means we must question the misleading ideas of conventional economics on what wealth-creating and wealth-consuming activities are. It is absurd, for instance, to accept that tobacco manufacture creates the wealth required to support the medical services needed to deal with lung cancer. And that is just one example of where we are led by those who tell us that conventional economic growth is a necessary prerequisite to social progress and so must be given priority over it.

We urgently need new indicators of economic, social and environmental well-being, as a basis for setting economic policy targets and for measuring economic achievements. The inadequacy of the Gross National Product (GNP) for these purposes is much more widely appreciated now than it was even five years ago. The GNP needs to be replaced, or at least supplemented, by more concrete indicators of the state of economic and social well-being and of the natural and man-made environment. The infant mortality rate and the under-5 mortality rate are good measures of the general health and well-being of a population.[4]

HEALTH, WEALTH AND ECOSYSTEMS: THE 1992 PROCESS

Over the past two decades—since the Club of Rome's first report[5] and the United Nations' Stockholm Conference of 1972[6]—awareness has been growing that the world faces serious environmental problems. During the 1970s and early 1980s the issue was commonly seen as being about trade-offs between environment and development—about reaching compromises between acceptable levels of economic activity and acceptable levels of environmental damage. By the later 1980s it had become more widely understood that, if economic activity is to become ecologically sustainable, a new marriage between ecology and development is needed. The Brundtland Report reflected this shift:

> Economics and ecology must be completely integrated in decision-making and law-making processes—not just to protect the environment, but also to protect and promote development. Economy is not just about the production of wealth, and ecology is not just about the protection of nature; they are both equally relevant for improving the lot of humankind.[7]

[4] See Victor Anderson, *Alternative Indicators*, Routledge, London, 1991.
[5] Donella and Denis Meadows et al. *The Limits to Growth*, Pan Books, 1972.
[6] Babara Ward and René Dubos, *Only One Earth*, Penguin, 1972.
[7] *Our Common Future*, Oxford University Press, 1987, pp. 37–8.

It was unfortunate that this call by the Brundtland Commission for a new direction—or new paradigm—of development was muffled and largely obscured by its simultaneous, more conventional call for a new era of economic growth. But at least the '1992 Process', leading up to the forthcoming U.N. Conference on Environment and Development in June 1992 in Brazil, is now focused on the need to deal with the worldwide environmental threats and the widespread failures of economic development as aspects of a single world crisis. That is useful progress in itself. A crucial part of the 1992 Process from now on must be to get it understood that conventionally measured economic growth is neither good nor bad in itself but is a meaningless target or measure of progress.

. So where does health come in? Brundtland made the right noises, at least so far as the Third World is concerned:

> Good health is the foundation of human welfare and productivity. Hence a broad-based health policy is essential for sustainable development. In the developing world, the critical problems of ill-health are closely related to environmental conditions and development problems...
>
> These health, nutrition, environment and development links imply that health policy cannot be conceived of purely in terms of curative or preventive medicine, or even in terms of greater attention to public health. Integrated approaches are needed that reflect key health objectives in areas such as food production; water supply and sanitation; industrial policy, particularly with regard to safety and pollution; and the planning of human settlements...
>
> Hence, the WHO Health For All strategy should be broadened far beyond the provision of medical workers and clinics, to cover health-related interventions in all development activities.[8]

This is good, as far as it goes. But two further points are outstanding. First, the need to integrate health, environmental and economic decision-making applies to industrialised countries, as well as Third World countries. Second, activists for 'the new public health'—including those involved in the WHO initiatives on health promotion and healthy public policies outlined earlier in this chapter—must find ways to engage effectively in the 1992 Process.[9]

EUROPE, AND THE CHALLENGE OF 1992

Parochial Europeans—from the business, financial, political, bureaucratic and professional classes—think of 1992 as the year in which the European

---

[8] Ibid., pp. 109–110.

[9] [1997 note. In the event, this hope was not realised. To date, the need to extend healthy public policy making beyond the boundaries of the professional 'health' sector is still unmet.]

Single Market is to be achieved. They are largely unaware of its wider historical significance.

1992 will be the 20th anniversary of the Stockholm conference on the environment. More importantly, the UNCED Conference in Brazil—the Earth Summit—will be the first time in human history in which representatives of all the peoples of the world will have come together to discuss our common future. Most significantly of all, 1992 will be the 500th anniversary of what, with engrained cultural arrogance, European peoples have been taught to think of as Columbus's 'discovery' of America. That event marked the beginning of the aggressive expansion of European Christianity and subsequently European secular culture all over the globe. This has led to the dominance of today's mechanistic, amoral, economistic worldview over those of other cultures. And it is that which now threatens the health and very survival of the human race and even of life on Earth. So 1992 will be an occasion for a worldwide reorientation of the most radical kind.

That, together with developments in Central and Eastern Europe and the Soviet Union—countries in which the links between health, economy and environment have become all too apparent—presents the peoples of Europe with a threefold challenge.

First, we must put our own house in order. This means switching to a new development path in Europe itself, in which the creation and maintenance of healthy living conditions for people and the restoration and maintenance of natural ecosystems are among the primary objectives of personal lifestyles, business strategies and economic policies. The principles evolved by WHO–Europe over the 1980s must be brought into economic decision-making.

Second, by making this switch ourselves, Europeans must offer to the rest of the world a new model of economic progress—much less rapacious and much more benign towards people and the Earth than the model we have propagated over the past half-millennium.

Finally, commonhealth has an international dimension. Europeans, in transforming our own economic order, must take a lead in transforming the present worldwide pattern of economic dominance and dependency between rich and poor countries—together with the UN, Bretton Woods and other international institutions that reinforce it. By helping to create a new, more equal system of economic relations, we will be helping today's poorer peoples to create healthy and sustainable economies, and healthy and sustainable natural environments, for themselves.

Cholsey, Oxfordshire
1991

10

Devil's Tunes

This chapter was first published under the heading 'An Infernal Strategy Review' in Sheila M. Moorcroft (ed.), *Visions For The 21st Century*, Adamantine Press, London, 1992.

January 1997

An Infernal Strategy Review

The attached document came to me recently without explanation, from a source which I have been unable to trace. It carries no date, but internal evidence suggests it was written in 1991. It embodies a vision for the 21st century—and beyond—which highlights the subjectivity of futures thinking. The future to which it is committed is not the future to which most of us look forward. On its own terms it is optimistic, but most of us may well draw pessimistic conclusions from its optimistic approach.

James Robertson
Cholsey, 1st April 1992

Top Secret Memorandum to the President

STRATEGY FOR THE NEXT CENTURY
AND THE NEXT MILLENNIUM

After the last Stygian Council meeting a hundred years ago, You asked us to review infernal strategy for the next century and the next millennium. This is a summary of our report. It is for discussion at the forthcoming Council meeting.

Since the Council first met several millennia ago we have steadfastly pursued the goal we then agreed. This was well summarised by a Mr. Milton in a report on those early events. That report, entitled *Paradise Lost*, is quite recent and You may not yet have had time to read it. Milton describes our aim as 'seducing the race of Man' into 'wasting God's whole creation' to the point where He 'with repenting hand would abolish His own works'—an accurate reflection of our self-appointed task.

We are able to report good progress over the past few hundred years. The cancerous impact of the human species on itself and on the ecosystems of the Earth has now well and truly taken hold—to the point where it could soon prove terminal. This offers us the prospect of an important victory over the Enemy. We can take satisfaction from it.

However, we must not be complacent. As increasing numbers of humans come to recognise the gravity of the world crisis they are creating (with our concealed assistance), they might be inspired to halt their stampede toward the abyss. They could still change direction just in time to thwart our Plan.

The following is a possible scenario. A United Nations Conference on Environment and Development is to be held in June next year in Brazil. This Earth Summit will be a historic event. For the first time ever the peoples of the world will meet together to discuss their 'common future'. And 1992 will be a historic year. It will be the 500th anniversary of Columbus's voyage to the Western hemisphere. That voyage marked the beginning of the modern Euro-American period of human history, which now promises to culminate in the global disaster for which we have been working. The suggestion is that, when such a historic meeting in such a historic year confronts humans with the occasion for worldwide reflection and repentance, this will bring them to their senses; and that then the approach of 'The Year 2000'. which many of them will see as the time for a millennial breakthrough, will strengthen their determination to switch to a different path of progress for the future.

We have examined this scenario and understand it, but we do not find it realistic. The pressures of career competition and survival in business and finance and politics and government around the world will almost certainly be strong enough to frustrate the success (from the human point of view) of the Earth Summit. Furthermore, in this as in other matters of concern to us, our infernal skills of disinformation and public relations will keep the professional communicators on our side. We can rely on the world's media to ignore the potential significance of the Earth Summit until it is actually taking place, and then to concentrate on its entertainment value rather than the serious issues at stake.

Nonetheless, we recommend that infernal observers watch very carefully the efforts humans make in the next few years to change their present path of development. We should continue to encourage them to play down the severity of the risks they now face. We should persuade them that prudence and good judgment call for delay until scientists and economists can agree on what needs to be done. (We can rely on economists to argue for many years about what 'sustainable development' actually means.) For the longer term we must make sure that the efforts that humans eventually make to achieve sustainability are positively counter-productive.

In that respect we must follow the pattern of our previous successes. We contrived to persuade humans to transform the Christian atonement of 2000 years ago into the service of their own material ambitions and struggles for power. We helped them to transform the initial journeys of Christian explorers from Europe 500 years ago into a worldwide wave of destruction, in which many peoples and cultures and biological species have perished—and continue to perish today. In the last two or three hundred years we have successfully encouraged them to transform the scientific revolution and the 'Enlightenment', on which they originally embarked with such high moral and spiritual purposes, into more powerful engines of physical and moral and spiritual destruction and waste than have ever existed before. We have helped them to redefine 'the creation of wealth' as a competitive struggle for supremacy and survival among themselves, and to redefine 'economy' as a compulsive addiction to unnecessary extraction and wastage of nature's resources.

These are no mean achievements. The challenge is to live up to them now. But this should not be beyond our powers.

Influential human leaders are already calling for 'a new wave of economic growth' to deal with the problems that past economic growth has caused. What might have been dangerous ideas like democracy and development have already been converted into instruments—like the 'free market' and 'free trade'—through which rich and powerful people can dominate and disable the poor and weak. In the last few years concern with sustainable development has itself mushroomed into an unsustainably wasteful bonanza of parasitical busyness—national and international conferences, consultations, publications, research, and so on. Mad scientists, dreaming of nuclear reactors in 50 years' time that will generate heat 2000 times hotter than the sun, are given serious attention; while sober engineers, capable of providing all the energy humans need by a mixture of energy efficiency, energy conservation and renewable energy supply, are dismissed as unreliable cranks. (Our experts from the Ministry of Destruction and Science and the Ministry of Disinformation and Public Relations are asking for increased budgets to step up their successful co-operation in this area.) Meanwhile leading humans, by simultaneously paying themselves huge salaries and preaching the virtues of wage restraint, elegantly combine encouragement of financial greed with the promotion of widespread cynicism. (You recently recognised the brilliance of our infernal taskforce in this area by bestowing a Satan's Award for Excellence on the relevant division in the Ministry of Waste and Economic Affairs.)

In these and many other ways things are going well. With discreet help from us, the human race seems hell-bent on its own destruction and the destruction, if not of a very large part of the Universe, of enough of the Enemy's creation to be well worth our while.

As You know, the question has been raised whether this would necessarily turn out to be a victory for us. Might not the self-destruction of the human species and its environment, like the past destruction of earlier species (e.g. the dinosaurs), help to create conditions in which new, more advanced forms of life and consciousness would eventually emerge on Earth? Might we not then feel that, far from our having triumphed over the Enemy, He had skilfully outmanœuvred us?

We reject that doubt for two reasons. First, more advanced forms of life and consciousness would, in fact, widen the future scope for infernal subversion of the Enemy's creation—*corruptio optimi pessima*, as His supporters say. That is an outcome we would welcome. Second, the disaster threatening the human species is now so imminent that their successful avoidance of it might well be interpreted as a defeat for us. That is an outcome we would want to avoid.

To conclude, then, our unanimous recommendation is that infernal strategy should encourage humans to continue on their present catastrophic course. We seek the Council's agreement and Your authority to proceed accordingly.

B. L. Z. Bubb	(Minister, Planning)
M. Ammon	(Minister, Waste and Economic Affairs)
M. O. Loch	(Minister, Destruction and Science)
B. E. Lial	(Minister, Disinformation and Public Relations)

11

Beyond Horseshit Economics

This chapter is based on the opening speech (and subsequent contribution to a panel discussion) at a conference in Berlin in November 1992 on 'Employment and Economic Regeneration In Crisis Regions'. The conference was organised for the Berlin City Government and the Technical University of Berlin by Dr Karl Birkholzer of the Institut für Hochschuldidaktik's Forschungsprojekt. The conference led to the setting up of the European Network for Economic Self-Help and Local Development.

The text was published in *Futures*, March 1993 under the title 'The Fallacy of Single-Level Control: Local Economies In A Changing Global Environment'. The reason for the new chapter title will become apparent.

January 1997

The Fallacy of Single-Level Control:
Local Economies in a Changing Global Environment

To be discussing new approaches to the economic problems of Berlin and the surrounding East German region in the aftermath of unification, on the spot with so many of the people directly concerned, is of special interest. But there is also a further significance to these proceedings. If Germany, so highly regarded for so long as a model of successful economic progress, is now beginning to focus on economic policy-making at regional and local levels within the national economy, economic thinkers and policy-makers in countries like Britain may at last begin to take this seriously too.

Local strategies for employment and regeneration in crisis regions raise questions that are more wide-ranging than might be apparent at first sight. These include questions about the further integration of national economies in the larger European economy, and about the further development of global economic structures. These national and supranational economic structures will provide the future framework of expectations, opportunities and constraints for local economic decision-making and local economic activity. Their nature will help to determine whether local economic measures continue to be seen as merely remedial and marginal, or whether economic policy-making at local level will come to be seen as an integral part of a new approach, multi-level rather than single-level, to mainstream economic policy-making.

Conversely, decisions on the future role of local economic policy-making will help to shape the new national and international structures which are now needed to foster equitable and sustainable world development—an issue which is still very much alive in spite of the failure of the Rio Earth summit in July 1992 to tackle it effectively. They will bear even more directly on the form which further economic integration in Europe is to take following the Maastricht Treaty.

THE HISTORICAL BACKGROUND

Centralisation has been a dominant theme in the economic development of industrialised and industrialising countries during the last two centuries.

135

Localities and regions have become increasingly dependent and vulnerable. They have become increasingly dependent, as if on absentee landlords, for employment and for goods and services (including financial services and welfare services) on large organisations—industrial, commercial, financial and governmental—whose main interests and decision-making headquarters are outside the locality or region. They have become increasingly vulnerable to economic decisions, economic policies and economic events outside local control.

During the 19th and 20th centuries economic orthodoxy crystallised around the assumption that economic policy-making is a matter for centralised national macroeconomic management. Micro-economics came to be about the behaviour of firms, not about local economies or the economies of local communities or households. And, until fifteen or twenty years ago, it was generally accepted—in Britain, at least—that local government had no economic functions. Local government's functions were limited to environmental and social matters like planning and housing. So far as economic policy-making was concerned, local and regional economies were regarded as more or less non-existent.[1]

One result of this process of national economic centralisation has been to reinforce economic imbalances within national economies—to widen the gap between richer, economically buoyant areas on the one hand and poorer, economically depressed areas on the other. For example, as national banking and financial systems became more centralised, they increasingly channelled savings out of depressed areas into investment in more active areas which offered a higher return. As national companies grew in numbers and influence, the development of their branch networks not only reflected but also helped to accentuate the shift towards economically active areas and away from depressed ones.

Most important in this respect has been the inflexibility of national macroeconomic policies, which control the availability of spending power and regulate the level of demand throughout the national economy. National economic policy-makers have always faced a dilemma. They can either aim to make enough spending power available to stimulate economic activity in the depressed areas of the economy, at the cost of inflating the economy as a whole. Or they can aim to avoid inflating the economy as a whole, at the cost of not making enough spending power available in the depressed areas to stimulate local economic activity there. They can very rarely achieve both the goal of controlling national inflation and the goal of stimulating the

[1] [1997 note. I still recall this as one of the points impressed upon me as a young Whitehall official in the 1950s.]

depressed parts of the economy. (Monetarists have leaned toward the first of these, controlling inflation. Keynesians have leaned toward the second, stimulating the economy. But both have faced the same dilemma.) The damaging effect of a single-level system of macro-economic control, and the need for a more flexible system of economic demand management, is a key point for the future. I shall come back to it later.

RECENT DEVELOPMENTS

From as far back as the 1920s and 1930s up to the present time—I am speaking here of Britain—there has been a continuing history of special policy measures with a confusing variety of different names and titles, aimed at providing remedies for the problems of depressed areas. They have not been successful, in the sense that no effective or lasting solutions have yet been found. However, in the last fifteen or twenty years the assumption that local economies have no existence and that local government has no economic functions has begun to be questioned. So far the questioning has mainly involved practical, piecemeal responses to local need and local crisis. A systematic new approach to the management of local economies has still to take shape. The more conventional type of response, on which much the most money and effort has been spent, has been externally orientated. Local authorities have accepted the dependency of the local economy on outside economic forces as a fact of life, and have looked to the outside world for the answers to their economic problems. They have competed with one another to make their region or locality financially, socially and environmentally attractive to national and multinational employers. This has led to various imaginative ideas and false hopes. Typical of these has been the idea of golf-course-led growth. The suggestion, seriously made by one of our British Ministers for Industry in the later 1980s, was that authorities in the North Western part of England should encourage the development of a number of world-standard golf courses to attract inward investment. These would attract senior Japanese businessmen to set up factories and offices in the area, and in due course jobs in them would trickle down to a number of people living in that part of the country.

The most spectacular recent failure of this externally orientated, trickle-down approach to the economic regeneration of depressed local areas in Britain has been Canary Wharf. It has been calculated that the greater part of £6,000,000,000 (six billion pounds sterling) of British taxpayers' money went into this top-down scheme, now bankrupt, to regenerate London Docklands. Little of it reached the people actually living there. Not only has it brought them little benefit. It has positively damaged local jobs, local housing, the local environment and local quality of life.[2]

Americans, too, are familiar with the efforts of local authorities and city governments to attract inward investment by outside business corporations in new factories and hi-tech plants in their areas. They call such efforts 'smokestack-chasing' and 'chip-chasing'.[3] I remember finding, on one visit to the United States about ten years ago, that almost all the towns I visited were hoping to turn themselves into the microchip manufacturing centre of North America. In Britain we are not quite so ambitious as that. Our depressed towns and districts tend to pin their hopes on tourism, museums and theme parks. But, unfortunately, whatever external source of salvation an economically depressed region looks for, there just is not enough potential inward investment, or enough demand for microchips, or enough tourists, or enough whatever else out there, to go round. In other words, it is only possible for this externally orientated approach to be successful in exceptional cases, not as a general rule.

This began to become apparent in the later 1970s and early 1980s. Another, more innovative, approach to local economic regeneration then began to attract increasing support. This approach is internally, not externally, orientated. It aims to mobilise unused local resources—especially unemployed people—to meet unmet local needs. It places the emphasis on fostering a greater degree of internal economic self-reliance, rather than renewing and reinforcing external dependency.

Initiatives of this type have mushroomed all over the industrialised world in the 1980s and 1990s. Nevertheless, they are still seen as exceptional and marginal so far as economic policy is concerned. They are not yet widely recognised for what they could turn out to be—first steps towards:

- a new perception of local and regional economies as distinct entities in their own right, each needing an autonomous economic policy-making capability of its own; and
- a new emphasis on greater local and regional self-reliance as an economic policy goal.

In short, the basic situation remains today much as it has been. In a centralised national economy, local economic regeneration is not seen as a goal of mainstream economic policy. It is still seen as remedial—a lifeboat operation to pick up some of the casualties that the centralised mainstream economy leaves in its wake.

[2] *All that Glitters is not Gold: A Critical Assessment of Canary Wharf,* Docklands Consultative Committee, Unit 4, Stratford Office Village, 4 Romford Road, London E15 4EA, May 1992, p. 1.

[3] David Morris, *New City States,* Institute For Local Self Reliance, Washington, 1982.

THE INTERNATIONALISATION OF ECONOMIC ACTIVITY

If that is the situation in a world of centralised *national* economic policy-making, how will it be affected by the increasing *internationalisation* of economic activity?

There is little doubt that further European economic integration, in the unitary form of Economic and Monetary Union and a single European currency as proposed in the Maastricht Treaty, would tend to reinforce the situation I have described. It would be a further measure of economic centralisation, accentuating economic imbalances between different regions of Europe. It would tend to worsen the prospects of the crisis regions. It would require a larger lifeboat operation to rectify the imbalances and remedy the crises in the economically disadvantaged regions. That is well recognised. The larger remedial role—the bigger lifeboat—is provided for in the Maastricht Treaty's proposals for a new Committee of the Regions and an enlarged European Regional Development Fund, together with the so-called Cohesion Fund.

One possibility for the future would be simply to accept this, to recognise that the present plans for European Economic and Monetary Union will create an even more urgent need to deal with a larger number of economic crisis regions. It would then be necessary to step up preparations to meet that need. But another possibility is to seek an alternative to the unitary form of European economic integration that is now proposed.

Let us be quite clear about what this means. To oppose a unitary form of integration does not mean opposing further European economic integration as such. Internationalisation is a feature of all aspects of human activity today, including economic development. That is a fact of life. Multinational corporations and multinational banks now affect us all. The impacts of economic activity in one country now affect others—just think of acid rain, or global warming, or Chernobyl. At the European level, closer economic cooperation has long been seen as a contribution to peaceful, secure relations between the peoples of Western Europe. At the global level, the need to evolve a more environmentally sustainable world economy, which will also be more equitable, calls for a new economic approach at the world level and for more effective world-level economic policies and institutions in the spheres of international trade, aid and finance.

So further internationalisation of economic structures, both in Europe and at the global level, is—in my view—desirable and inevitable. The important question is what form it should take, and what should be the guiding principles underlying it.

139

TWO GUIDING PRINCIPLES

There should be two main guiding principles.

The first is the democratic principle. Must the process of internationalisation make the exercise of economic power still more undemocratic? Must it make people in localities and regions even more dependent than they now are on remote economic institutions over which they have no control? Must it make them even more vulnerable to economic decisions taken without regard to their own local and regional circumstances? Or can the process of economic internationalisation be accompanied by a process of economic decentralisation and economic democratisation? Can the European Community principle of subsidiarity be applied in the economic sphere? In other words, can we organise for economic decisions to be made and economic controls to be exercised at the closest possible level to the people affected by them? Instead of arguing whether centralised economic powers should or should not be transferred from the national level to the European level, can we begin to evolve a multilevel structure of economic policy making and management—local, national, international? Can we arrange for policy decisions affecting the economic interests specific to us, as Berliners or Londoners, or as Germans or British, or as Europeans, to be the responsibility of democratically controlled government authorities at each of those levels?

The second guiding principle is the principle of economic rationality and efficiency. The key point here is the irrational and inefficient effects of a single-level system of macro-economic control.

THE INFLEXIBILITY OF SINGLE-LEVEL CONTROL

A single level of control cannot be flexible enough to manage a complex system efficiently. This is well recognised in engineering systems design. It is well recognised in business management, where the decentralisation of decision-making to profit centres and cost centres within a framework of overall corporate control is now the norm. It is not yet recognised by mainstream economists and economic policy-makers. The following story may make the point clearer.

Once upon a time it is taken for granted that chickens can be allowed to feed only from the grains of corn they can find in horse manure. The result is that to give their chickens enough to eat, farmers must give their horses too much; and, when they stop giving their horses too much, their chickens get too little. Farm management policy is in a stop-go trap, for ever doing U-turns between giving too much corn to horses that are already too fat, and allowing too little food to chickens that are already too thin. Farming experts argue constantly on TV and radio and in the papers about what should be done. Some favour giving the horses too much—they call it 'going for growth'. Others favour giving the chickens too little—they say that if the policy isn't hurting it isn't working. Some propose breeding a more competitive and enterprising strain of chicken. Others propose what they call 'supply side' action to change the digestive system of horses. All agree that the chickens need better education and training. But all these sophisticated experts miss the point, which is so simple they cannot see it. The point is that when the amount of food available to chickens depends on the amount given to horses, it is impossible for both to get the right amount.

However, the story has a happy ending. One farmer's little son secretly allows his father's chickens to forage for food that has not had to 'trickle down' through horses. Horses and chickens both flourish on that farm. In due course, the little lad confesses and the truth becomes known. Eventually, in spite of resistance and all manner of far-fetched explanations from the experts, the conventional wisdom shifts. It becomes accepted that a single-level system of control, determining how much food is supplied to chickens by how much is given to horses, is not after all a rational and efficient system of farm management. Decoupling control of chicken food from control of horse food gives better results all round.

The truth[4] is that a single level system of control—whether in a farm, in a business or in an economy—cannot avoid imposing dependencies and rigidities which are highly irrational, dysfunctional and inefficient. When applied to the former centrally planned economies of the Soviet Union and Eastern Europe, this has always been widely regarded as obvious. But, as I have said, most economists and economic policy-makers still fail to recognise that it applies to the macro-economic management of capitalist market economies too.

So let me underline the point yet again. An efficient and rational economy that facilitates the use of available resources to meet needs that would otherwise remain unmet must be flexible. It must decouple the control of what needs to be controlled locally from the control of what needs to be controlled nationally, and it must decouple both of these from the control of what needs to be controlled at a supranational level.

---

[4] A more important truth, according to one American reader of the *Futures* article when it was published, is that much conventional economics is 'horseshit'. Hence the new title of this chapter.

A MULTI-LEVEL APPROACH

I suggest, then, that we need to explore the possibility of further European economic integration—and, beyond that in due course, the further development of global economic policy-making institutions and instruments—on a multi-level basis and not a unitary basis. We need to explore how a multi-level structure of economic policy-making might work, with each level exercising the economic controls appropriate to its area— supranational, national or subnational—according to the specific needs of the area in question.

It would imply, to take one example, that instead of aiming to replace national currencies with a *single* European currency which everyone in Europe would be compelled to use, we should introduce—at first on an experimental basis—a *common* European currency to be used alongside national currencies by those who would find it useful to do so. Moreover, it would imply that city and other local authorities should be allowed to issue their own local currencies or quasi-currencies—means of local purchasing power—to be used alongside the national and European currencies if they thought it necessary to make new local spending power available in their locality to enable unused local resources to be employed to meet unmet local needs.

This is not the place to discuss the details or argue the merits of such a multi-level currency system. I mention it, not because I think it is an idea that will carry general agreement today. (If I were asked to guess, I would say it might be another four or five years before it comes on to the mainstream political and economic agenda.) I mention it to illustrate the fundamental nature of the changes likely to be needed, if the evolving framework of international and national economic decision-making is to become more, rather than less, supportive to regional and local economic regeneration.

The same principle can be illustrated by considering the role of the household in the economy. In reconceptualising the economy as a multi-level system and restructuring economic activity on a multi-level basis, we need to include the household level as well as the supranational, national, regional and local levels. We need to recognise, as conventional economic theory and policy-making today do not, that the household—like the subnational region or locality—is an economic entity that either produces wealth and well-being or fails to do so. More rational economic policies for the future will then aim to enhance the capacity of households—as well as of localities, regions and nations—to create wealth and well-being. The economic role of the household must be an important item on the new economic agenda for subnational regions and localities.

This will have radical consequences. Recognising the economic role of household workers will call in question the conventional assumptions that the basic productive unit in the economy is the firm (company), and that the only 'economically active' work is work done by employees for employers. The assumption that people must depend for work on the amount of employment generated by employers will then be seen for what it is—another example of the   chickens-must-depend-upon-what-trickles-down-through-horses syndrome. That false but largely unquestioned assumption now provides the basis for policy across a wide range of fields—including employment, education, training, social security, taxation, housing, environmental planning and industry. It is the root cause of the unemployment problem, and it contributes to a range of personal and social problems and tensions connected with the economic and work roles of women and men in modern industrial societies. In this context it was interesting to find that the same department of the Berlin city government is responsible both for Employment and for Women's Affairs.

ENVIRONMENTAL SUSTAINABILITY IN A MULTI-LEVEL SYSTEM

It will be clear, I hope, that adopting a multi-level rather than a unitary approach to closer international economic cooperation would open the way to systematic local and regional policy-making as a positive aspect of mainstream economic policy.

Local and regional economic policy-making of that type would give more attention than today to:

- ways in which a greater proportion of local needs could be met by local work using local resources;
- ways in which a greater proportion of local income could be encouraged to circulate locally, instead of leaking out of the local economy; and
- ways in which a greater proportion of local savings could be channelled into local investments or loans, in order to contribute to local economic development.

Many local and regional economies would clearly have the opportunity to become more sustainable than they are today, in the limited sense of becoming more self-reliant and less vulnerable to economic decisions and policy changes and events outside their control. But this new approach to local economic policy making would encourage them to become more environmentally sustainable too.

143

In the first place local economic policy-makers, in pursuing the three points mentioned above, would, for example, encourage energy conservation and, where this is possible, the use of local energy sources to meet a greater proportion of local energy needs. That would reduce the dependence of the local economy on outside energy sources, and increase the proportion of local income and expenditure available to circulate locally. As a spin-off, it would also contribute to environmental sustainability. Encouraging more recycling of local waste is another policy that would contribute both to greater local economic self-reliance and to environmental sustainability. In suitable localities and regions, increasing the proportion of local food consumption met by locally produced food could do the same.

Energy, waste recycling and food are just three examples of many possibilities for local import substitution that systematic new strategies for increasing local or regional self-reliance would be able to pursue. And, of course, the overall volume of goods transported between localities will be lower, if localities generally become more economically self-reliant than today.

But, secondly, beyond these particular contributions to environmentally sustainable development, which would come about as spin-offs from the pursuit of greater local economic self-reliance as a policy goal, we should also envisage the emergence in the coming years of a policy-making structure at national, European, and United Nations levels that will, among other things, increasingly encourage environmentally sustainable development at every level. Within that new multi-level framework, it will become a positive aim of policy-making, at subnational levels as at others, to encourage environmentally sustainable patterns of activity.[5]

A TWIN-TRACK APPROACH

In conclusion, then, we should recognise that further international economic integration is desirable and inevitable. But we must ensure that this does not result in the further centralisation of an already overcentralised unitary system of economic policy-making and management. On the contrary, the internationalisation of economic policy-making must be accompanied by decentralisation of economic functions to subnational regions and localities. Innovative arrangements to liberate them from out-of-date rigidities in the economic system will be an essential counterpart to further international

[5] [1997 note. This now happening in an increasing number of local areas under Local Agenda 21 programmes initiated as a result of the 1992 Earth Summit.]

economic integration.

A twin-track, simultaneously internationalising and localising, approach of this kind will enable the peoples of Europe to pursue still further their post-war vision of peaceful economic cooperation. It will mean that further European economic integration can become democratic and decentralising. It will enhance overall economic efficiency. It will encourage local enterprise. It will positively help all those who are grappling with the persistent problems of crisis regions, instead of making their task more difficult. And it will be a key element in evolving the new global policy-making structures which will be needed to foster more environmentally sustainable economic development worldwide.

Cholsey, Oxfordshire
1992

12

Monetary Democracy for Europe

This chapter was published under the heading 'Economic Democracy: A Multi-Level System Of Currencies' in *New European*, Vol. 5, No. 2, 1992, edited by John Coleman, 14–16 Carroun Road, London SW8 1JT.

It takes forward the discussion in Chapter 11 about a multi-level approach to the evolution of a one-world, decentralising economic system, and develops the case for a multi-level system of co-existing currencies as part of it.

Since 1992, the arguments for such an approach have become more widely understood. In particular, interest has grown in the spread of Local Exchange Trading Systems (LETS) which, at the grass-roots level, enable local people to club together to exchange goods and services with one another and to keep score, without having to acquire national currency in order to do so. But the important potential role of local currencies more generally is also becoming increasingly understood.[1]

January 1997

---

[1] [1997 note. An excellent account of LETS and other local currencies will be found in Richard Douthwaite, *Short Circuit: Strengthening Local Economies for Security in an Unstable World*, Green Books, 1996. Its two chapters on 'Cutting the Monetary Tie' and 'Banking on Ourselves' run to 117 pages.]

Economic Democracy
A Multi-Level System of Currencies

Can the dynamic of economic integration in Europe become democratic and decentralising, instead of bureaucratic and centralising? Can it help to foster local enterprise and local economic autonomy, instead of increasing the dominance of multinational businesses and banks? If it is to do so, it will have to include—among other things—the development of a multi-level system of co-existing currencies.

In addition to existing national currencies this will involve the creation of a common, as opposed to a single, European currency—broadly on the lines of the British Treasury's proposals of November 1989. But it will also involve something neither the British nor any other European government has seriously contemplated yet—the emergence of city and other local currencies at the subnational level.

These co-existing European, national and local currencies will have to be flexibly but coherently articulated with one another within an integrated European framework. But before going into the details, we need to look at the context—both at the sub-European national level and at the supra-European global level.

First, then, let us remind ourselves that, within the nation, the conventional national monetary system based on a single national currency has a centralising and dependency-creating effect. In essence this effect arises whenever the need is imposed on people to obtain money from sources outside their own collective control in order to secure their livelihood and enter into economic transactions with one another. From earliest historical times those with power have used money this way as an instrument of domination and exploitation. By taxing subsistence farmers, ancient kings—like modern colonial rulers—compelled them to work as paid labourers for larger landowners, since that was the only available source of money to pay the taxes. Just so, today's centralised national monetary system artificially restricts economic autonomy and freedom within the nation.

A single national currency for the whole of Britain means that the economic activities of the inhabitants of a city like Liverpool, suffering from economic decline and high levels of unemployment, have to depend on inflows of the national currency, which their depressed circumstances make it very difficult for them to earn. Under a single national currency they depend on inflows of it, not only to provide them with the external purchasing power to import goods and services from other parts of the nation or from abroad— which is reasonable enough. They also need them because they have no local source of internal purchasing power to support purely internal economic activity within the local economy of the city itself. And that, when you think about it, is not at all reasonable.

Why, then, are Liverpudlians not allowed to issue their own city currency as a medium of exchange to support economic transactions between themselves within their own city? Such a currency might not be readily accepted or highly valued elsewhere, but it would certainly provide a means of reviving and supporting the internal city economy. Exactly the same goes for the inhabitants of other comparable cities in Britain, and in other countries too.

The answer is that there is no reason in economic logic or equity as to why cities should not issue their own currency. Tiny nations, like the Seychelles, far smaller in population than Liverpool, issue their own currency and prosper the better for it. The main reason why city currencies are not allowed is that the national government, national banks and national businesses want to keep their dominant power of external control over the internal economic activities of the nation's cities.

It may seem strange that, with one or two shining exceptions like Jane Jacobs in *Cities and the Wealth of Nations*,[2] so few professional economists and monetary and financial experts have questioned this in the past. The fact is that the great majority have identified, most of them no doubt unconsciously, with the centralising tendency of their employers, who have almost always been national and supranational government agencies, business corporations and financial institutions, or universities, research institutions and journals parasitic on those agencies.

As we approach 1994, the 300th anniversary of the birth of the modern national monetary system with the founding of the Bank of England in 1694, we must bring this and other aspects of conventional monetary orthodoxy increasingly under the spotlight. This will help to stimulate more thoughtful discussion about the monetary aspects of further economic integration in Europe than we have seen hitherto.

Turning now to the supra-European context, it is striking how parochial and Eurocentric the approach to European monetary integration has been so far. It is as if none of the well-paid people responsible for it has been aware of

[2] Jane Jacobs, *Cities and the Wealth of Nations*, Penguin, 1984. See also David Weston on 'Money and Our European Environment', in *New European*, Vol. 3, No. 6.

the integrative pressures also bearing on the international economy at the global level. As I pointed out two years ago in *New European*,[3] the increasing urgency of global ecological problems, the growing hold of transnational corporations on economic life, the global impact of the Third World debt problem, the emergence of a one-world financial system based on computer communications between Tokyo, London, New York and other financial centres, and the increasing need for international consensus on the policies of organisations like the IMF, the World Bank and the GATT, all emphasise the need to develop a measure of economic integration, and the new institutional structures needed for economic policy and management, at the global as well as the European level. The necessary institutional innovations must eventually include some form of global currency or quasi-currency to replace the US dollar, whether developed out of Special Drawing Rights—as was once expected—or via some other route.

The need for a more integrated global framework of this kind, within which the nations of the world—rich and poor alike—can be encouraged to switch to a sustainable direction of development, seems bound to emerge even more clearly when the Earth Summit—the UN Conference on Environment and Development—achieves either success or failure in Brazil in June this year. But even five years ago, when the Brundtland World Commission reported in 1987 on *Our Common Future*, those whose job it was to formulate sensible directions for European economic integration, might have noticed the wider context in which further European integration would be taking place.

If they had noticed it, they might have paused to consider whether their approach to European integration would make sense if extrapolated to the global level. In that case they would hardly have thought of proceeding on the simple assumption that the right way forward involves the progressive transfer of functions, such as issuing a currency, from lower to higher levels— from the national to the continental level today and, according to the same logic, from the continental to the global level in due course. The prospect of 80% of all important economic decisions in Europe being taken in Brussels, and the inhabitants of John o' Groats being forced to use the same currency in their corner shop as the people of Herakleon in theirs, delighted Jacques Delors. He might have been less enthusiastic about the prospect of that being merely a staging post *en route* to 80% of all the important economic decisions in the world being taken in a single centre, and of the inhabitants of Paris being forced to use the same single global currency as the inhabitants of Papua New Guinea, Murmansk, Milton Keynes and Timbuctoo.

[3] *New European*, Vol. 3, No. 1.

Quite clearly the right question is not whether particular economic and monetary functions should be transferred from one level to another—from national to European, and in due course from European to global. The right question is how these functions are to be carried out at each level of a multi-level one-world economic system designed to be positively decentralising and empowering, and how they are to be articulated between one level and another. So, how to proceed?

The first step is simply to accept, with an open mind, that a multi-level system of co-existing currencies might perhaps be worth taking seriously as a possible feature of further economic integration.

The next step is to hypothesise how such a system might be developed. For example, each level of government, European and local (where a local government authority wished to do so), might be encouraged to issue its own means of payment (an embryo currency) in parallel with existing national currencies, and to use it in payments to and from itself. Banks and other financial institutions might be expected to handle accounts denominated in these new currencies, as well as in existing national currencies. All organisations and individuals would be free to decide which currencies to use in transactions with one another, and to operate bank accounts in whichever currencies they wished.

Taking this or something like it as a starting point, the next step will be to carry out detailed studies, including computer simulations, on how such arrangements could actually be expected to work, what their implications might turn out to be, and what variations on them might be desirable. For example, a question to be considered will be whether it should be open to governments (at European, national and local levels) to regulate or to tax currency exchange transactions in any way, or whether such transactions should be left to the operation of an entirely free market in currencies. This process of study and simulation can be expected to lead to some modifications and refinements of the original proposals, and eventually to a set of workable proposals which, after exposure to public discussion and debate, and given the political will, could be progressively introduced.

I am confident that work on these lines will be done in the next year or two, perhaps not by the governmental monetary authorities or commercial financial institutions who might be expected to do it, but by pioneering bodies such as the New Economics Foundation and others like it. It will be an important practical contribution to the vision needed, but so far largely lacking, as a guide to further economic integration in Europe.

Cholsey, Oxfordshire
1992

13

After Keynes and Thatcher: What Now?
An Open Letter to the Chancellor of the Exchequer

This chapter was first published in *Resurgence*, May/June 1993, under the title 'The Keynes and Thatcher Revolutions Have Both Failed: What Now?'. Norman Lamont was Chancellor of the Exchequer at the time.

I had for some time been aware of the arguments for combining the introduction of a Citizen's Income with radical tax reform, including energy and environmental taxes. Being commissioned to write this article by the editor of *Resurgence*, Satish Kumar, spurred me to explore the topic in greater depth. In 1994 the New Economics Foundation published a pamphlet of mine called *Benefits and Taxes: A Radical Strategy*. Chapter 16 below, on Citizen's Income and Radical Tax Reform, published in the *Political Quarterly* in January/March 1996, developed the discussion further. More recently, in November 1996, in connection with my Visiting Fellowship at the Green College (Oxford) Centre for Environmental Policy and Understanding, I helped to convene a seminar on this subject under Sir Crispin Tickell's chairmanship.

January 1997

The Keynes and Thatcher Revolutions have both Failed: What Now?

An Open Letter to the Chancellor of the Exchequer

Dear Chancellor,

We are not making a very good fist of managing our economic affairs. You may not admit this publicly, but in your heart I am sure you agree.

After all, it isn't just a question of your personal competence, or the competence of your particular party. There is no politician, no party, no established school of economic thought, that knows how to do much better. The state of the art is backward.

Even if some shoots of short-term recovery are now visible, we have very little room for manoeuvre over the next few years. It's the same old story. As far back as most of us can remember, we have been caught in the Stop-Go trap. Our only options have been policies that would stoke up inflation, policies that would deepen recession, and U-turns between the two.

Keynesian policies, by pumping up demand, have led to runaway rises in wages and prices. Monetarist policies—reducing demand by keeping interest rates up and public spending down—have raised unemployment and set back the economy as a whole. Prices and incomes policies negotiated by government with industry and the trade unions to keep costs stable have simply not worked.

In the last few years, membership of the European exchange rate mechanism (ERM) tightened this trap. European Monetary Union and a single European currency system à la Maastricht would tighten it further. Being forced to leave the ERM was a blessing, at least in the short term. But simply reverting to national economic management on the old model won't get us far.

So, what are we to do?

I believe the time has come to change economic goals altogether and aim for a new path of economic progress—more ecologically sustainable, more socially just, more concerned with quality of life than with conventional economic growth. But I wouldn't dream of trying to persuade you of that. You and your Cabinet colleagues and your Treasury advisers, and, for that matter, your political opponents and their advisers, dismiss ideas like that as irrelevant. You would throw this letter straight in the bin marked 'Greens, Third World do-gooders, New Age weirdos, etc.'

No, my suggestions to you are more in tune with accepted traditions of economic analysis and Conservative party thinking. Their aim is to improve economic efficiency:

- first, by removing obstacles to the more efficient use of the three traditional factors of production—labour, land and capital,
- and second, by evening out the Stop-Go cycles.

WHY KEYNES AND THATCHER BOTH FAILED

Following the slump of the 1920s and 1930s, many people hoped that John Maynard Keynes (1883–1946) had found a way forward. He recognised that rigidities and blockages had developed in the economy, such as organised wage-bargaining by trade unions and monopolistic price management by big business. Whatever might have happened formerly, the frictionless adjustment of wages and prices to supply and demand that would—according to classical economic theory—automatically restore the economy to equilibrium at full employment, no longer took place. Positive intervention was needed to pull the economy out of recession.

Keynes focused on a blockage that impeded the efficient use of capital. Saving and investment were no longer automatically matched to one another by supply and demand as classical economic theory assumed. Those who saved were now a different group of people from the entrepreneurs who invested. At times of recession, savers would have a high propensity to hoard the money they saved, i.e. to keep it liquid and out of circulation. The rate of interest necessary to persuade them to lend their savings to investors would be higher than the interest which commercial investors would be willing to pay, given the low prospective return on investment at such times. How, then, could investment, incomes and demand be restored to a level that would get the economy going again?

Keynes' answer was that government should fill the gap with publicly financed investment programmes. For a time many people hoped that this would work. But once the exceptional war-time and post-war 1940s and 1950s were over, that hope proved unfounded. Keynesian policies kept up employment only by keeping inflation up too. The rigidities that made the economy malfunction could not, after all, be effectively by-passed or neutralised by the kind of intervention Keynes proposed. So by the late 1970s the time had come to try again to restore free-market flexibility and enable the economy to function more nearly according to the classical economic model. That has been the aim of Conservative governments since 1979.

Unfortunately, neither you and the other ministers in these governments, nor the free-market economists who have advised you, have appreciated how far-reaching a thoroughgoing free-market approach would have to be. For all the sound and fury surrounding your labour legislation and denationalisation programmes, they have been too narrowly focused. Let me explain.

Paradoxical though it may seem, the Thatcher revolution is failing for much the same reason as the Keynes revolution failed. It has concentrated on only one of the three factors of production. The Keynesian strategy operated on the availability of capital in the hope that intervening to bypass the blockage there would be enough to make the whole economy function more efficiently. The Thatcherite strategy has concentrated on labour in the hope that removing blockages to more flexible employment would do the trick. The hope in both cases has proved vain. The lesson seems clear enough. It is necessary to operate on all three factors of production, to remove blockages to the more efficient use of all three. The five proposals that follow for fundamental changes in the social security and tax systems are designed to meet that need. A good deal of work has been done already on each of these by different expert groups. I suggest that you should consider combining them.

WORK

PROPOSAL 1. A CITIZENS' INCOME. As many existing social benefits as possible, including unemployment benefit, child benefit and state pensions, should be consolidated into a basic monthly income paid unconditionally to all citizens.

PROPOSAL 2. TAXES. Income Tax (including National Insurance), Value Added Tax (VAT), and Company Profits Tax should be phased out.

Artificial obstacles now prevent a match between the potential supply of work and the potential demand for it. They keep people idle instead of enabling them to do work that clearly needs to be done. These obstacles arise from the existing social security and tax systems, and the assumptions underlying them.

You will notice that I have called this factor of production 'work', not 'labour' as economists normally do. This is because we must now question the assumptions that:

- people should normally depend on employers to organise their work and provide their income, i.e. give them a job;
- paid work is more valuable than unpaid work; and
- paid work is the only work that need concern economic policy makers.

Perhaps it is not surprising that in their time Keynes, and late Beveridge, failed to question dependency on employers as the norm. But you and your Conservative colleagues in the 1980s and 1990s might have been expected to do so, given your much proclaimed aversion to the 'dependency culture'. However, you seem to have been bothered only by dependency on government and trade unions. You seem to have had no objection to people being dependent on employers to provide them with work—nor, for that matter, being dependent on big business and big banks.

My first and second proposals, then, are aimed at removing features of the social security and tax systems that both

- discourage employment of the conventional kind, resulting in many millions of people in this and other European countries now being unemployed; and
- discourage people from engaging productively in the unpaid family and neighbourhood work of the household and the local community.

A Citizens' Income will improve economic efficiency in a number of ways:

- It will allow many people to undertake useful work who are now kept idle by the unemployment and poverty traps. These often compel unemployed people to keep themselves available for jobs which don't exist, or mean that, if they do start working, they will lose more in lost benefits (and tax) than they will earn.
- By enabling people to negotiate with employers on a more equal footing, it will permit a freer labour market, thus improving the efficiency of business and industry. On the one hand, normal levels of wages and salaries may tend to fall. On the other, potential employees will be better placed to demand higher pay for unpleasant work.
- It will liberate people to do useful unpaid work in their households and neighbourhoods. It will raise the work status of family care and care in the community.
- Finally, by cushioning people against the downswings of the Stop-Go cycle, it will help to stabilise the economy.

The Citizens' Income should be paid for by new land and energy taxes as will be discussed below. A full Citizens' Income could not be paid for out of Income Tax or VAT without raising those taxes to levels that would stifle economic enterprise and efficiency.

Even at present levels, these taxes penalise the results of work. They skew the economy against work in favour of capital-intensive forms of production. Income tax, in particular, creates disincentives to work, including the poverty trap. Together with company profits tax, it discriminates against household production in favour of business production, because households have to buy their productive equipment out of taxed income whereas businesses do not. In effect, value-added tax too is largely a tax on work. Its cumbersome administrative requirements are economically wasteful. They penalise small enterprises in particular. Finally, these taxes generate an amount of tax avoidance activity which is unproductive and economically inefficient. They should be replaced with new taxes on land and energy, to which I now come.

LAND AND ENERGY

PROPOSAL 3. LAND TAX. A tax on the unimproved value of land, or a site-value rent, should be phased in, as existing taxes are phased out under Proposal 2. (Eventually, this tax could also replace this year's new Council Tax, with a proportion of the revenue from it going to local government.)

Distortions affecting the economically efficient use of land—i.e. the matching of the potential supply of land to potential demands for it—are hardly less serious than those affecting work.

Most of the reward from land now goes to those who hold it, while many of the associated costs do not. Activities of the community as a whole raise site values in a locality, but the capital gain on each particular site goes to its owner. It often pays landowners to keep valuable sites unused, in order to sell them later when their value will have risen. Speculation on rising land values distorts land prices, generally making them significantly higher than they would otherwise be.

This puts land out of reach for many potential users and uses, and puts housing out of reach for many people who need it. It also amplifies the turbulent effect of Stop-Go cycles. When recession comes, the slump in land and property values can be devastating—as many young people will testify today who, having bought their first home, now find themselves with negative equity, i.e. debts greater than the value of their property.

As a general rule, the site-value tax will not raise production costs (which may fall as a consequence of Proposal 2), because landowners will be unable to pass the tax on to land users. That is because, in a market economy, the price that land users can pay for land is limited by the production costs they can afford and those in turn are limited by the prices people are prepared to pay for what the land users produce. In practice, no doubt, landowners will try to recoup some of the tax by raising the prices of the products and services they themselves produce (as land users) and by raising their rents to tenants. They may succeed to some extent owing to imperfections in the market. But the most important effects of the tax will be to reduce the unearned element in incomes which land owners now get from its profitable use, and to increase the costs of land owners who keep their land out of use or use it unprofitably.[1]

This will tend to bring about an overall reduction in the capital value of land, making it available for people and purposes not able to get it now and generally encouraging more economically efficient use of land. By reducing the scale of speculative capital gain (and loss) from land, it will also help to damp the swings of the Stop-Go cycle.

PROPOSAL 4. ENERGY TAX. A new tax on energy should be phased in, along with the new tax on land.

Energy is the other basic natural resource, along with land, that enters into all or virtually all economic activity. It must now be treated as an aspect of the factor of production traditionally known to economists as 'land'.

Like the proposed land tax, the new energy tax will be levied at the point where energy first enters the economic system, i.e. at source. It will then cascade down through the economy, tending to raise the price of all goods and services with a high energy content and to reduce all salaries, wages, dividends, capital appreciation, etc., that derive from high energy use. It will encourage the efficient use of energy, just as the new land tax will encourage the efficient use of land. (It will also, of course, tend to reduce the total use of energy and the pollution that energy-intensive activities create.)

Revenue from the new land and energy taxes will have to finance the additional government spending needed for the Citizens' Income, as well as replacing revenue from the taxes being phased out. So the levels at which they will have to be set will be fairly high.[2]

CAPITAL

PROPOSAL 5. A CURRENCY EXCHANGE TAX. A tax on currency exchange transactions should be introduced. This could be set at 1% of their value.[3]

[1] This paragraph is a revised version of the original one, which was misleading.

[2] [1997 note. Illustrative calculations were included in my booklet *Benefits and Taxes: A Radical Strategy*, New Economics Foundation, 1994.]

Distortions now affect the economically productive use of capital no less than labour and land. And these distortions also make a major contribution to the turbulence of the Stop-Go swings.

95% of the foreign exchange transactions in London have nothing to do with trade in real goods and services. The overwhelming emphasis on making capital gains and avoiding capital losses can result in spectacular ups and downs, as on Black (or Golden) Wednesday last September.[4] The same goes for the stock exchange and other financial markets. Channelling savings into new investment in productive activities plays a very small part. The great majority of capital transactions take place in the secondary market—i.e. the buying and selling of already existing assets like stocks and shares.

The more efficient use of work and land and energy will itself make for more efficient use of capital. It will encourage people to invest their savings in enterprises and activities in which work, including their own work, plays a major part. It will help to reduce the attractions of speculative capital gain. And it will damp the volatility of capital asset values and the turbulence of Stop-Go swings. So the proposed tax on currency exchange is the only measure I wish to suggest now specifically to promote the more efficient use of capital.

This tax will provide some disincentive to currency speculation. It will bring in revenue, in addition to the new land and energy taxes, needed to replace the taxes being phased out. It will also encourage import substitution and greater economic self-reliance. But that raises large questions about the future of the international economy, including the future of the European Community after Maastricht. And those are not the subject of this letter.

More far-reaching changes in the monetary and financial system, involving the 'denationalisation' of money, would also encourage the more efficient use of capital. Moreover, there may be a case, once the five proposals I have put forward have been implemented, for removing all taxes on capital gains and capital transfers. But each of those is another very large topic, which I cannot cover in this letter.

[3] [1997 note. Such a tax is often known as Tobin Tax—after James Tobin, the Nobel-Prize-winning economist who first suggested it. A much lower rate of tax is suggested by those who view the purpose of a Tobin tax as simply to raise revenue to finance the United Nations, rather than to dampen speculation and provide an effective buffer or threshold between national and international (and between local and national) economies. For discussion of the issues at the international level, see the Report of the Commission on Global Governance, *Our Global Neighbourhood*, Oxford University Press, 1995, p. 219; and *Futures*, Vol. 27, No. 2, March 1995, Special Issue on 'The United Nations at Fifty: Policy and Financing Alternatives'.]

[4] [1997 note. In September 1992 speculation against sterling forced its withdrawal from the European Exchange Rate Mechanism (ERM) and its devaluation. The day became known as Black Wednesday, except by those who saw sterling's devaluation as a boost to British exports and the British economy as a whole. They called it Golden Wednesday. Many still see that way.]

CONCLUSION

You will now be starting to think about the second 1993 Budget, a historic event when—for the first time ever—the government will be looking at its spending and revenue proposals together. I congratulate you and your colleagues on this long overdue reform. It makes it possible to consider a combined programme of spending and tax changes on the lines I suggest.

Phased in over a period of years, these changes will help to create a much freer and more efficient market economy. Of course, there never could be such a thing as a totally free market. The way a market behaves is inevitably shaped by the government-created framework of laws and regulations, taxation and public spending, existing at any particular time.[5] But the changes I am proposing in the framework will lead to greater economic freedom and efficiency. For that reason I imagine you may be sympathetic to them.

If you wish to take them forward, the first step will be to ask your officials to examine their implications. What would the overall picture of government spending and revenue look like, given the Citizen's Income on one side and the new pattern of taxation on the other? At what levels would the Citizen's Income and the new land and energy taxes be set? What problems of administrative feasibility would have to be overcome? What would be the main effects on economic activity? What would the international repercussions be? How fast might it be possible to phase in the whole programme?

I am sure this is the way into the future, and out of the Stop-Go era. I very much hope you will be prepared to take the first steps along it. As it happens, it will also contribute to environmental sustainability, social justice and quality of life. But just count that as a bonus. It may bring you votes from circles which do not normally give you support.

With best wishes
James Robertson
January 1993

[5] [1997 note. There is also the fact that, if a totally free market economy were ever to exist, it would increasingly find itself dominated by an increasingly small number of increasingly powerful players who would diminish and then destroy the freedoms of other less powerful people and organisations. The free market would automatically transform itself into one that was unfree.]

14

What's Wrong with Nuclear Power?

For many years I have understood why so many people are so strongly opposed to nuclear power, and I have shared that point of view. My vision of a more self-reliant sane, humane and ecological (SHE) future has included the liberation of people and local communities from our present degree of dependence on large, remote, nationally and internationally controlled sources of energy supply, 'whether dominated by coal miners, nuclear engineers or oil sheikhs'.[1] I have felt that the prospect of a world dominated by nuclear power reflects all that is wrong with the vision of a hyper-expansionist (HE) future. It epitomises the drive to perpetuate the dependency culture. I still hold that point of view today.

This chapter was written for the Churches' Energy Group in September 1993 as a discussion paper on 'Some Arguments Against Building More Nuclear Power Stations'. The Group had been convened so that supporters and opponents of nuclear power could discuss together how the world's needs for energy could best be met, recognising that we were 'all deeply concerned to protect our home—planet Earth—from a threatening catastrophe'. The hope was that this might make it possible to narrow the areas of disagreement. The chairman was Sir Frank Layfield, who had chaired the long-running public enquiry that led to the government's 1987 go-ahead for the Sizewell B nuclear power station. The convenor was Bishop Stephen Verney. The executive secretary was Peter Saunders, a public relations official (and latterly an independent consultant) in the nuclear industry.

A selection of the Group's papers, under the title 'Energy', was published as the Winter 1993 issue of *Christian Action Journal*. However, by then the internationally respected environmentalist Diana Schumacher and I had regretfully left the Group. We felt that it was failing to give sufficient emphasis to the questions of social, political and ethical principles and values which we felt were important. In retrospect, it may have been unrealistic to hope that a group of people with such strong pro-nuclear and anti-nuclear commitments could reach agreement.

---

[1] [1997 note. See Chapter 3 above.]

What's Wrong with Nuclear Power?

I have been asked to cast this note in negative form: Why should more nuclear power stations NOT be built. Let me first summarise the positive choice from which that negative follows.

It is necessary to develop new ways of enabling everyone in the world's growing population to meet their energy needs, while drastically reducing worldwide emissions of greenhouse gases from fossil fuels—including reducing CO_2 emissions to about 10% of the present UK per capita level in the next fifty years. The right way to do this is by:

- improving energy efficiency;
- changing to less energy-intensive patterns of progress; and
- developing the use of renewable energy sources.

As well as phasing out fossil fuels, the strategy should include:

- building no more nuclear power stations;
- phasing out existing nuclear power stations; and
- decommissioning them and cleaning up the nuclear detritus left over from the past forty to fifty years.

That is the right course not just in the UK itself. By taking it, we will help to lead other countries in the right direction. In commercial terms we will develop capabilities in energy efficiency, renewable energy supply and nuclear clean-up, for which worldwide demand will continue to grow rapidly.

AN END TO NUCLEAR POWER

There are many reasons for phasing out nuclear power.

NUCLEAR POWER IS NOT NECESSARY. Independent experts (e.g. from the Stockholm Environment Institute) are quite clear that fossil fuels do not have to be replaced by nuclear power. They have shown that 60% of the world's needs can be met by renewable energy by 2030 and 100% by 2100, and that nuclear power can be phased out by 2010. (This is regarded as unnecessarily slow by scientists working for bodies like Greenpeace and Friends of the

Earth.) There is now clear scientific evidence that phasing out nuclear power as well as fossil fuels is technically and economically feasible. The question is about the will to do it.

NUCLEAR POWER IS A DISTRACTION. The overriding priority is to develop energy efficiency, energy-conserving patterns of progress, and renewable sources of energy supply. Building more nuclear power stations would falsely imply that that cannot meet the need, and would weaken the sense of urgency and political commitment for it. The divisive effect of continuing controversy over nuclear power would further distract attention from it.

NUCLEAR POWER DENIES THE NEED FOR REPENTANCE. Entrusting a significant future role to nuclear power would be a form of escapism. It would encourage the belief that humankind can continue on its present course regardless: produce more, consume more, put our faith in technical fixes; escape the personal and political responsibility of deciding to change direction; dismiss theological talk of repentance or 'metanoia' as irrelevant to the real choices of real people living real lives.

ARE ARGUMENTS IN FAVOUR OF NUCLEAR POWER OBJECTIVE? This must also be questioned. Here are some of the reasons why this is the case:

- Most people who advocate nuclear power have a specific connection with nuclear science or the nuclear industry. They profit from it, are paid by it, make a career in it, or have spent their life's work in it. Few of those who, even as independent external inspectors, are qualified to pronounce on the technical safety of nuclear power, would be thus qualified unless they had committed their working lives to the nuclear field. By contrast, many of those who question nuclear power do so as citizens, in support of no specific material interest or personal commitment of their own. That their part is David's against Goliath will have struck anyone attending a public enquiry.
- Strong emotional commitment drives those who argue for nuclear power. Nuclear spokespeople suggest that they deal in objective facts, and their opponents in subjective fears. The converse is just as true: they rely on subjective hopes, against which their citizen opponents produce objective facts.
- The case for a continuing worldwide role for nuclear power ignores evident objective facts about human behaviour and fallibility. It presupposes a make-believe *Dr Strangelove* world, where everything is

strictly controlled by highly trained, tidy-minded, impeccably behaved, professional scientists and engineers working in laboratory conditions.

Plain common sense requires us to question the objectivity of 'expert' views on many of the following points.

SAFETY RISKS. Statistics today can calculate the risks only from the historical record so far. But the risks for the future are of huge disasters, rising dramatically if worldwide use of nuclear power were to grow. Not just operating risks. Risks, for thousands of years, from the impact on nuclear installations of terrorism, war, civil unrest, management breakdowns, corruption, and many other forms of human fallibility—let alone unpredictable natural hazards like earthquakes and volcanos.

HEALTH RISKS. The long-term health risks of future worldwide use of nuclear power could not be responsibly assessed until after several more generations at the earliest.

FUTURE GENERATIONS. It is wrong to impose on future generations problems and costs which will last for thousands of years and risks which we cannot now evaluate.

RISK EVALUATION. In every field of science and technology, people are increasingly unwilling to accept risks which experts declare to be 'safe enough' or 'as low as reasonably achievable'—ALARA, in their professional jargon. People note that the acceptable safe limits of exposure to harmful substances are revised downwards as the years pass, and that scientific interventions often go wrong. Well-known examples in the medical field include thalidomide, fertility treatments, cancer misdiagnoses, and blood transfusions for haemophiliacs. Distrust of expert judgement is particularly strong where nuclear power is concerned, partly because of the magnitude of the potential disasters when the scientists and engineers get it wrong.

MILITARY SPIN-OFF. An expanded world role for nuclear power would be bound to increase the risk of proliferation of nuclear weapons, and their availability to terrorists and madmen. Nuclear experts argue that it is technically difficult to make nuclear weapons from materials and equipment needed for nuclear power generation. Whatever the truth of that, it misses the point. In the real world as it is, effective international surveillance to prevent proliferation of nuclear weapons would be seriously weakened if every potential Saddam Hussein could legitimately claim possession of large quantities of nuclear materials and equipments. (Remember how supergun components for Saddam Hussein were nearly passed off as oil pipework?)

HIGH-LEVEL SECURITY REQUIREMENTS. These involve a degree of security and secrecy that fosters complacency, poor management, dishonesty, failure of accountability, and other symptoms of a potential Big Brother state. This may have been particularly evident in the former Soviet bloc. But the nuclear industry's record elsewhere has already led many people to a similar conclusion—not just because of false financial costing, misinterpretation of scientific data and concealment of accidents, but also over its links with private and public security and intelligence agencies. There have even been suggested links with violent crime in Britain and the USA. Karen Silkwood's death is a well known example from the USA. In Britain, a suggested explanation for the unsolved murder of Hilda Murrell was that she could have been the victim of a botched surveillance operation linked with her opposition to Sizewell B—or alternatively with her nephew's part in the Belgrano controversy. Whatever the truth about that particular case, the fact that people found such an explanation plausible speaks for itself.

FINANCIAL COSTS. It has been calculated that, when all the relevant costs of nuclear power are counted in—including R & D (research and development), planning and construction, operation, insurance, waste disposal, and decommissioning—they are greater than those of any other method of meeting energy needs. Although such calculations can be disputed, e.g. by imaginative estimates of global warming costs attributable to fossil fuels, the facts speak for themselves. First, the eventual costs of nuclear power will not be known for thousands of years, until no more expenditure is needed to deal with its wastes and any future hazards they may cause. Second, so far as the present situation is concerned, the UK private sector was unwilling to take over nuclear power stations at the time of privatisation, when—for the first time—the real costs became widely understood.[2] Now, contrary to the free-market philosophy that the present UK government would apply if it could, the state-owned nuclear operators are heavily subsidised. They are guaranteed against having to meet 'unexpected' costs associated with decomissioning existing power stations and the management of spent fuel and nuclear waste. They are guaranteed against having to meet liabilities of more than £20 million in the event of accident. They are guaranteed that the grid will take all

---

[2] [1997 note. This refers to the original privatisation of the electricity industry as a whole. More recently, the newer nuclear power stations have been privatised. The price at which the government was able to sell them was massively written down in comparision with their original cost.]

the electricity they can produce. They receive an annual subsidy of £1.25 billion, costing electricity users a 10% addition to their electricity bills. And government R & D spending (1990 figures) on nuclear energy is £115 million, contrasted with £14 million on energy conservation, £16 million on renewables, and £11 million on fossil fuels.

ENERGY BUDGET. It has also been calculated that the energy budget of nuclear power yields a deficit, in other words that nuclear power uses more energy than it produces. The total amount of energy used to research, develop, build, operate and decommission a nuclear power station and manage its wastes will be greater than the amount of energy the power station can generate during its operating lifetime. Again, as with financial costs, calculations of this kind can always be disputed. What cannot be disputed is that nuclear power compares unfavourably in terms of its energy budget with other ways of meeting energy needs. The 'payback period'—how long it takes for the energy produced to exceed the energy used—for wind energy, for example, is very short. The payback period for nuclear power will not be finally established for thousands of years, when no more expenditure of energy is needed to deal with its wastes and whatever hazards they may cause.

THE THIRD WORLD. The Third World does not need nuclear power to meet its energy needs. There is even greater scope there for solar, biomass and other renewables, together with energy efficiency and conservation, than in the 'developed' world. The Third World only needs nuclear energy like it needs imported tobacco products—to keep Western multinational companies in business. There is a particularly insidious form of neocolonialism here. Those who support nuclear power argue that it has proved to be so dangerous and expensive in the former Soviet bloc—despite well-developed capabilities in science and technology—due to the bad management of nuclear power stations. How, then, would the good management of an increasing number of nuclear power stations be ensured in countries all round the world that do not have those capabilities? Who would build, manage and control them? And how would they be financed? There could be only one answer. They would be built, managed and controlled by multinational companies, and they would be financed by even higher levels of Third World debt than those that cripple Third World economies today. (The Bataan Nuclear Power Plant in the Philippines can be cited as an example. Built by an American company on an earthquake fault for $2.2 billion amid accusations of fraud, it remained idle while costing the Philippine people $355,000 per day in foreign debt interest payments. When eventually—in 1992—debt relief proposals were offered, they were conditional on the Philippine government's abstention from taking the American multinational company to court.)

POLITICAL. Nuclear power is politically divisive. That is an objective fact about the real world. It cannot be wished away by hopes about nuclear power's potential to achieve satisfactory technical performance in a make-believe world. Wise leaders and responsible citizens avoid gratuitous political conflict when—as in this case—an alternative course of action is available.

MAINTAINING A NUCLEAR ENERGY CAPABILITY. Some nuclear advocates claim that, even though new nuclear power stations are not needed, some should continue to be built in order to maintain the capability to build them, in case that capability might be needed at some future date after all. This argument ignores the following points:

- A substantial nuclear energy capability will be kept in being, whether new power stations are built or not. Its task, for which it will have to keep up with the crucial aspects of the state of the art, will be to deal with the still outstanding challenges posed by nuclear waste disposal and decommissioning.
- Any new power stations that were to be built in the UK in the foreseeable future would not be of British design. We are already dependent on imported know-how.
- The principle of continuing to do something for which there is no foreseeable need or demand, in case the ability to do it might possibly be needed some time in the future, belongs more to the political economy of *Alice in Wonderland* than to the free market. It could be applied to almost anything anyone cared to suggest.

SUMMING IT ALL UP

Nuclear power is unnecessary. It exemplifies many of the sinful and ungodly features of the present approach to economic development worldwide— addictive and exploitative, dominating and dependency-reinforcing, unecological and spiritually arrogant. Repentance lies in a new commitment to a new direction of sustainable development. We must give high priority to giving up nuclear power.

September 1993

15

Social Investment

A key feature of the dependency culture is the assumption that savers and investors should depend on financial experts and financial institutions to decide how their money should be used—to what kinds of people and companies it should be lent, in what kinds of initiatives and projects it should be invested. Just as the dependency culture expects people to hand over to employers the responsibility of deciding the purposes of their work, so it expects them to hand over to bankers and fund managers the responsibility of deciding the purposes to which their money should be put.

Recent years have seen a significant growth in ethical investment and social investment. In a negative sense, this is about people deciding not to allow their money to be invested in businesses of which they disapprove, such as the arms, tobacco and alcohol industries. In a more positive sense, it is about people deciding to invest in activities or companies which they positively want to support, such as the development of new environmental technologies like wind-power, or enterprises committed to fair trade with Third World producers, or companies with fair and equal employment policies. The growth of institutions that enable people to invest according to social and environmental, ethical and political, values is an important feature of a society beginning to throw off the dependency culture.

This chapter takes further the discussion of a number of points raised in Chapter 7. It contains the text of the opening talk at a conference on 'Developing Social Wealth: Financing The Social Economy' held in Birmingham in May 1995. The conference was organised by the UK Social Investment Forum (UKSIF) and the International Association of Investors in the Social Economy (INAISE).

January 1997

Investing to Create Social Wealth

Rather more than ten years ago I did a study on 'Finance for Local Employment Initiatives' for the OECD and Directorate-General V of the European Commission. So it is good to see DG V represented here today. That study confirmed, for me, the importance of the idea of investing to create social wealth.

Then, in a 1987 paper on *Socially Directed Investment: and its potential role in local development,* I wrote:

> We have to envisage the possibility that a "third sector", consisting of enterprises with mixed economic and social objectives, will emerge alongside the conventional public and private sectors as a major feature of the 21st-century economy, and that with it will evolve a "financial third sector" alongside conventional public sector and private sector finance.[1]

And later, in *Future Wealth,*[2] I wrote:

> Investment to create social and environmental wealth will have a vital role in the new 21st-century economic order. An important strand in 21st-century economics will be to develop the practice and theory of social and environmental investment. New criteria and procedures for evaluating, accounting and auditing such investment will have to be worked out. New institutions will be needed to enable people...to channel their savings into this kind of investment.

My sense of the need to develop social investment to create social wealth has become even stronger since then, and I have no doubt of the importance of the pioneering role of INAISE and UKSIF in this field. Later speakers will be discussing specific aspects of investing in the social economy, so I want to say something about the broader context in which social investment may develop in the coming years.

---

[1] This paper was written for a New Economics Foundation conference at Wadham College, Oxford, in 1987 on 'Converging Local Initiatives', the convergence being between economic, social, environmental and financial initiatives.

[2] *Future Wealth: A New Economics for the 21st Century,* Cassell, 1990, p. 16.

THREE DIFFERENT VIEWS OF SOCIAL INVESTMENT

There are different views about the potential of social investment. I am not talking here about the different perspectives of:

- individual investors;
- public sector and governmental agencies;
- non-financial private-sector businesses and corporations;
- private-sector financial institutions; and
- third sector bodies (voluntary, non-governmental, etc.).

Social investment does, of course, mean something different for each of these groups:

- for individuals and third sector bodies (like churches) social investment means opportunities to invest in enterprises and projects they think worthy of support;
- for the public sector it means opportunities to use public expenditure more productively than on conventional social spending on welfare; and
- for private sector enterprises it means mainly—at least at the present time—opportunities for cost-effective promotional expenditure on 'public relations' and 'community affairs'.

But I would like to return to my topic—different views about the potential future significance of social investment for mainstream economic and social life.

VIEW I. MARGINAL, REMEDIAL—AN ALTERNATIVE TO CHARITY OR WELFARE. This is the view taken until recently by most business people, financial people, economists and policy-makers. They recognise that a comparatively small number of non-conforming individuals wish to invest 'ethically', in order to support enterprises and projects they think worthy of support. They also recognise that some public sector support for, say, community enterprises in areas of high unemployment may be a more cost-effective use of public money than welfare benefits. And they recognise that business and financial corporations are prepared to channel part of their promotional budget into social, including local community, projects. But they see ethical investors as a marginal minority interest (more concerned with charitable giving than proper financial investment), they see the social investment of public funds as a temporary short-term remedy for exceptionally high unemployment in particularly badly affected areas, and they see business spending on social investment as ancillary, and not integral, to mainstream profit-making business activity. In short, they do not see social investment as a potential feature of mainstream financial and economic life.

VIEW II. LONG-TERM, TRANSFORMATIONAL. This is a more visionary view. It holds that we are entering a period of transition from the modern age to a post-modern age, which will be characterised by people-centred development. Our ideas about work and money, and the way we use them and organise them, will change profoundly—as will other aspects of life and thought. This view sees today's conventional approach to investment, aiming for purely financial returns regardless of other considerations, as unsustainable for the long term. As we shift to a new path of sustainable, people-centred development, the proper function of money and finance will come to be seen as serving the needs of people and reflecting their values— including investing in the creation of social wealth and the conservation and restoration of environmental wealth. The objectives, the institutional structure, the control and the operation of mainstream monetary and financial activities will evolve in adaptation to that new perception of their function.

VIEW III. SOCIAL INVESTMENT AS AN IMPORTANT FEATURE OF CONVENTIONAL ECONOMIC REVIVAL. This view falls between the other two, it recognises that national (and European) economic performance and competitiveness in a globalised economy will be seriously handicapped by the economic and social costs of poverty, exclusion and high unemployment, and also by the costs arising from inefficiency in natural resource use and high levels of pollution and waste. In this view, conventional economic success and the financial returns it brings continue to be seen as the goal. But investment to reduce the social and environmental costs which prejudice that goal is seen as a necessary means towards it. Social investment is therefore seen, though in a supporting role, as an integral part of an efficient, globally competitive national or European economy.

I shall now say more about the second of these three views—the visionary, long-term, transformational view. Its perspectives will become more widely influential as time passes. However, we must recognise that, for the time being, most policy-makers, business leaders and economic advisers will not be able to accept it as a basis for policy. So I shall end by suggesting that, at least for the next year or two, the social investment agenda should focus on the practicalities of getting social investment established as an integral, though still supporting, element in mainstream economic policy. This will be a step forward from seeing it as only marginal and temporary. And it could be a transitional step towards eventually seeing it as a central feature of a new people-centred economy of the future.

PEOPLE-CENTRED DEVELOPMENT AND THE POST-MODERN TRANSITION

By people-centred development I mean an approach to development that enables people to develop themselves in ways that preferably enlarge, and certainly do not diminish, the capacity of other people to do the same. I distinguish it from business-centred, profit-centred, growth-centred, employer-centred or state-centred development, all of which can be hostile to development for people. But I do not see it as distinct from ecologically sustainable development. People-centred development and ecologically sustainable development are necessarily interdependent.

You can see them both as aspects of post-modern development. The modern age culminated in the impersonal structures of state socialism and financial capitalism—both very damaging to people and to the Earth. The breakdown of state socialism does not mean the triumph of financial capitalism and 'the end of history'. On the contrary, the removal of the threat posed by state socialism has brought into sharper focus the unacceptable features of financial capitalism. We can now question more freely our subordination to business and financial markets (as well as to the state). We can now see more clearly the potential importance of civil society as distinct from both conventional big business and the state—of civil society as a third sector in which citizens join together to act on behalf of themselves and other citizens.

There are many features of the post-modern transition that we cannot discuss here. The shift to a new post-European era in world history is one. The impact on literature and the arts is another. The breakdown of the modern ideas of scientific objectivity and the pursuit of certainty is yet another. But post-modern perspectives on work and money are directly relevant to our discussions today, and I shall say something about them.

A post-modern perspective on work recognises that a particular organisation of work is a basic feature of a particular kind of society. In ancient societies like classical Greece and Rome, most people worked as slaves for masters. In medieval European societies—feudal societies—most people worked as serfs for lords. In modern industrial societies, most people have worked as employees for employers. The work relationship has reflected the basic division of all those societies between a class of rulers and a class of ruled. But the division has softened at each stage.

Our vision of a post-modern society is of one in which the organisation of work no longer reflects a class division of that kind. Most people will no longer be expected to depend on employers to organise their work and provide their incomes. It will have become normal for people to work for themselves and one another, either as individuals or as members of self-managing groups and enterprises. The modern age of employment will have given way to the post-modern age of 'ownwork'. From being employer-centred, work will have become people-centred. An important task for social investment during the transition to a post-modern society is to enlarge the opportunities for people-centred ways of working.

A post-modern perspective on money will recognise that money has played the dominating role in late modern society that religion played in the late Middle Ages.[3] Then the local church was the most prominent building in most villages; today the prime sites in every high street are occupied by branches of banks, building societies and other financial concerns. The centres of medieval cities were dominated by cathedrals; today's city centres are dominated by the tower blocks of international banks. Today's army of accountants, bankers, tax-people, insurance brokers, stock jobbers, foreign exchange dealers and countless other specialists in money, is the modern counterpart of the medieval army of priests, friars, monks, nuns, abbots and abbesses, pardoners, summoners and other specialists in religious procedures and practices. The theologians of the late Middle Ages have their counterpart in the economists of the late Industrial Age. Then they argued about how to measure the space occupied by angels; now they argue about how to measure unemployment, the cost of living and the money supply.

At the time of the Protestant Reformation in 16th century Europe, the Church was experienced by increasing numbers of people as having lost its meaning, being out of control and operating in a thoroughly exploitative way. Just so, the money system is increasingly experienced around the world today as unreal, incomprehensible, unaccountable, exploitative, and out of control. Why should people lose their houses and their jobs as a result of financial decisions taken in distant parts of the world? Why should the international trading and financial system involve the systematic transfer of wealth from poor people to rich people? Why should someone in Singapore be able to gamble with our money on the Tokyo stock exchange and bring about the collapse of a bank in London? Why, when taking out a pension plan or a mortgage, should people have to rely on advice corrupted by the self-interest of the advisers? More and more of us are finding a financial system which works like this increasingly intolerable.

---

[3] [1997 note. This paragraph also appeared in Chapter 7. I ask readers to forgive the repetition. To have omitted it in either place would have risked interrupting the argument.]

SOME POST-MODERN PROSPECTS FOR MONEY AND FINANCE

So what changes could the post-modern transition bring in how we see money and how we deal with it? The following points will attract increasing attention.

MONEY BRINGS POWER AND RESPONSIBILITY. How we spend our money and invest our savings helps to shape our society and our world by channelling resources in some directions rather than others. Ethical consumerism and ethical investment recognise that people have a responsibility to use their money power, if they can, to support what they think is right and not what they think is wrong, and thus to help to create the kind of society and the kind of world they would like to see. New banks and investment funds will continue to develop, and existing financial institutions will continue to develop new services, to help people to spend and invest their money in accord with their ethical values.

WHAT IS THE MONEY SYSTEM FOR? How we spend and invest our own money is only part of the picture. It won't make much impact if the monetary, banking and financial system as a whole works inefficiently or unfairly or corruptly. More and more people in the coming years are going to be asking what it is for. What functions do we need it to perform? The short answer, of course, is that we need it to enable us to carry out economic transactions with one another and provide ourselves and one another with greater security for the future. Money and finance do this by providing a system of linked accounts (and also cash in the form of metal and paper tokens). These enable people to transfer financial claims between one another, either in exchange for goods and services now or in exchange for other financial claims entitling us to goods and services in the future.

The money system should be designed and operated to perform that function efficiently and fairly. Since we need the money system as an accounting (or scoring, or information) system, we should now evolve it purposefully to operate well as such. It should operate primarily in the interest of those who need to use it, and not of those who manage it—as it does now.

MONEY HAS NO EXTERNAL, OBJECTIVE VALUE. Historically, our experience of money, and of the whole system of money and finance, is of something provided externally to us by kings and governments and financial institutions. Culturally, the tendency of the modern age—supported by Adam Smith and other economists—has been to assume that money numbers (i.e. prices) should objectively reflect 'real values'. (There is a parallel here with the tendency of modern science to assume that numerical data objectively reflect real facts.) The post-modern perception of the world—and here there is a direct link with what it means for literature, the arts and science—is more subjective: to an important extent we create our own pluralistic realities. Just so, more and more of us will come to see money as an instrument developed by people for people's purposes. The idea will come to seem archaic and absurd that there could only be one kind of money—a single currency—at a national or even European or perhaps eventually a global level, and that monetary and banking experts—working like a priesthood or scientific elite whose arcane methods we cannot understand—should be entrusted with keeping money values in line with some kind of objectively existing numerical values out there.

THE MONEY SYSTEM IS OURS. In this context Local Exchange Trading Systems (LETS), though in practice still very small, embody an insight of great importance: that money is essentially something we can create for ourselves to facilitate exchanges between us; and that, although we may need someone to manage and operate the money system for us as bankers now do, the system is ours—to be managed and operated on our behalf.

WHY HAS THE MONEY SYSTEM NOT BEEN REFORMED ALREADY? The historical explanation for this is straightforward. The primary interest of the goldsmiths and bankers and government servants who have evolved the monetary, banking and financial system over the centuries, and the primary interest of the great majority of the bankers and other financial specialists who manage it today, has been to make money for themselves and their organisations, their customers, shareholders and other associates. Nobody has ever been responsible for seeing that the monetary, banking and financial system as a whole works efficiently and fairly for all its users.

CONCLUSIONS

The idea will become increasingly influential, I am sure, that social investment is one aspect of people-centred money and finance—and that people-centred money and finance are themselves an integral part of the people-centred development that will be a characteristic of the post-modern age. But, as I have said, these ideas are unlikely to be accepted as a basis for mainstream economic policy or theory in the immediate future. The main challenge, at least for the next year or two, will be to develop the practical implications of treating social investment as a continuing and necessary supportive element in conventional mainstream economic policy, rather than just as a matter of marginal or temporary concern.

This will mean securing greater support for a wide range of social investment activities and projects—from individual people, from the public sector at national and European level, from the national and international business and financial communities, from economic and social commentators, and from the media more generally. Moves in this direction are, in fact, already visible. Let me mention a few recent ones that come immediately to mind:

- the merger of Mercury and Triodos Banks to create a transnational social bank, and the launch of their new Wind Fund to enable people to invest in renewable energy developments;
- the launch of the Local Investment Fund by Business in the Community, as a partnership between the UK government and the private sector and to be managed by ICOF (Industrial Common Ownership Finance) and Lancashire Enterprises as a pilot project towards developing a national network of community development loan funds;
- the launch of the Aston Reinvestment Trust in Birmingham, to channel socio-economic development funds into a deprived part of the city; and
- the growing support of local government authorities for banking and money services, like credit unions and even LETSystems, for people who tend to be ignored by the conventional banking system.

For the future we must look, not only to many further developments of this kind throughout Europe, but also to some of the more wide-ranging changes in public policy now being canvassed. For example:

- changes in taxation—reducing the costs of people's work by shifting the burden of taxes away from it and on to the use of energy and resources and pollution, thus encouraging investment in work-intensive activities and services;
- changes in social benefits—using them as social investments, for example, to enable people to build up their skills and earnings by working in community enterprises without the disincentive of being worse off through loss of benefits; and
- encouraging the introduction of parallel currencies (at local as well as national and European level)—to provide local means of exchange in support of local activities while avoiding the risk of contributing to national inflation. This approach entails a common European currency

that people can use when they find it convenient, and not a single European currency that everyone has to use on all occasions.

Most of the discussion at this conference will rightly concern the practical questions and problems of social investment as it is today. But I hope that, as background to the discussion, we will have in mind the longer-term perspective and the possibility that what today we have to call the social economy may one day become the mainstream economy of the future.

Birmingham
May 1995

16

A New Social Compact

This chapter was published in *The Political Quarterly*, January/March, 1996. It was one of four contributions in that issue of the journal to a 'debate' on the subject of Citizen's Income, arranged by the editor, David Marquand. The other contributors were Ronald Dore, Philippe van Parijs and A. B. Atkinson. It is one of several articles I was writing for various journals about that time on the topic of tax reform and Citizen's Income.

Writing the *Resurgence* article reprinted in Chapter 13 above stimulated me to prepare similar evidence for the Labour party's Commission on Social Justice[1] and then to research:

- *Benefits and Taxes: a Radical Strategy*, a discussion paper sponsored by the Environmental Research Trust and published in 1994 by the New Economics Foundation; and
- *Electronics, Environment and Employment: Harnessing Private Gain to the Common Good*, a paper commissioned by Sir Crispin Tickell, director of the Green College (Oxford) Centre on Environmental Policy and Understanding, and published in *Futures*, June 1995.

The *Political Quarterly* article reprinted here owes much to the work I had done on those longer papers.

January 1997

---

[1] The Report of the Commission on Social Justice (the Borrie Commission) was published as *Social Justice* by Vintage in November, 1994.

A New Social Compact:
Citizen's Income and Radical Tax Reform

For radical reform to happen, certain conditions are necessary. Enough people must find the existing state of affairs unacceptable. Enough people must share a vision of a better state of affairs. If enough people can also see how to move toward that better state in good order—by evolution, not revolution—then reform is well on the way.

In this article I discuss the proposal to introduce a Citizen's Income as part of a radical package of changes in today's systems of taxation and welfare benefits—changes that will reflect and embody a new social compact between citizen and society. There is already widespread awareness that changes are needed. The challenge is to create agreed understanding of the form they should take and of how they can be brought in over a period of time.

A Citizen's Income (CI) will be a tax-free income paid by the state to every man, woman and child as a right of citizenship. The amount will be tied to the cost of living, but will be unaffected by a person's other income, wealth, work, gender or marital status. It will be age-related: higher for adults than for children, and higher for elderly people than 'working-age' adults. CI for children will replace today's child benefit, and CI for the elderly will replace today's state pensions. In principle, CI should replace all other existing benefits (and also tax allowances). In practice, supplements will be required to meet exceptional needs such as disability, and—at least for the foreseeable future—housing costs for low-income families.

Up to now, most CI supporters and researchers have assumed that CI would be financed out of income tax. But this would require excessively high levels of tax on all income other than CI—perhaps as high as 70%. And it is becoming increasingly clear that the prospect is for lower, and not higher, levels of income tax in all industrialised countries. That is one of the reasons why proposals for CI have to be considered along with proposals for tax reform.

Radicals can claim a respectable pedigree for the approach discussed here. As Stephen Quilley has noted in a recent issue of *Citizen's Income Bulletin*, Tom Paine (1737–1809) put forward an embryonic scheme to combine a Citizen's Income with a tax on land two centuries ago. In 1797, in *Agrarian Justice*, Paine argued that every proprietor of land should pay a

185

ground rent to the community. From the national fund so created, every person should be paid fifteen pounds on reaching twenty-one, 'as a compensation, in part, for the loss of his or her inheritance by the introduction of landed property', and every citizen over fifty should receive a pension of ten pounds a year. The proposals I discuss here are based on the same principle—of charging for the use of 'commons', in the sense of common resources and values created by nature or society at large, and of distributing a share of the revenue to all citizens as a right.

PRESENT PROBLEMS AND RECENT DEVELOPMENTS

Awareness in industrialised countries has been growing that our existing systems of taxes and welfare benefits are perverse—economically inefficient, socially unjust and divisive, and ecologically damaging. Taxes on incomes, employment, profits and added value penalise the contributions which people and organisations make to society. They tax people on the value they add, not on the value they subtract. By raising the costs of employment, they increase the level of unemployment, thereby causing waste of human resources and many social problems.

By contrast, the value that people subtract by using resources created by nature (such as energy and the environment's capacity to absorb pollution and waste) or by using values created by society (such as land values) is largely untaxed. This encourages inefficiency and waste in the use of natural resources. It allows private profit to be made from publicly created values (as, for example, the value of economically attractive city centre sites).[2]

So far as welfare benefits are concerned, not only is their total cost rising out of control. The present benefits system accentuates the perverse effects of the tax system. If people on benefit start earning income from work, they lose a corresponding amount of benefit. If, in addition, they have to pay National Insurance contributions and possibly income tax as well, they can suffer an actual reduction in income. This provides a powerful incentive for unemployed people, even if they want to do useful work, to stay unemployed—trapped in exclusion and poverty.

The existing benefits system also discourages saving, because people with financial assets are ineligible for benefits. People who have carefully saved, especially out of low incomes, thereby disqualifying themselves from receiving benefits, resent seeing more spendthrift people enjoying them.

[2] [1997 note. For example, when the route to be taken by the new Jubilee Line as part of the London Underground was announced, the value of properties near it went up without the owners of the land in question having done anything at all.]

Replacing means-tested benefits by CI would get rid of all these problems.

In the last few years, growing interest in 'ecotaxes' to support a shift to environmentally sustainable development has not only brought out the arguments in favour of higher taxes on pollution and the use of energy and other resources. It has also highlighted arguments for using ecotaxes to replace existing taxes. Continuing high unemployment calls for taxes on employment to be reduced or abolished. The need to attract inward investment in an increasingly competitive global economy also calls for lower taxes on employment, incomes and profits. And, as populations continue to age, it will become socially more divisive to tax the incomes of fewer people of working age, in order to provide pensions and care for the growing number of the elderly.

Economic studies in Germany, the USA and Switzerland, as well as the UK—and policy statements by the European Commission—are making it clear that, quite apart from the environmental and social gains, the replacement of existing taxes by new ecotaxes—shifting taxation off 'goods' on to 'bads'—can provide a double economic dividend. On the one hand, it reduces the distortionary effects of existing taxes. On the other, it provides financial incentives to use natural resources more efficiently.

Among recent studies particularly relevant to the linking of CI with ecotax reform is one that examined the effects of introducing an energy tax and returning the revenue from it partly to firms as a reduction in employers' social insurance contributions (in effect a reduction of tax on employment) and partly to private households as an 'ecobonus' (in effect a small Citizen's Income). It concluded that this would have positive economic effects, be conducive to employment, would not endanger national (German) competitiveness, would be progressive in the sense of reducing the net tax burden for households with low incomes, and could be introduced in one country without transgressing European Union rules. Another 'ecobonus' study (from Switzerland) concluded that, if the revenue raised from a levy of 2 Swiss francs per litre of petrol were distributed among all adults, people who drove less than 7,000 kilometres a year would benefit and people who drove more would lose.

ARGUMENTS FOR COMPREHENSIVE REFORM

A danger to be avoided as the need for changes in existing taxes and benefits becomes more widely accepted, lies in the fact that these changes themselves may proliferate piecemeal, promoted by different government departments separately responsible for employment, welfare, environment, economic competitiveness, and public revenues and expenditures, with no overall strategy for the development of the combined system of taxes and benefits as a whole. Such a proliferation of new overlapping taxes and charges, tax rebates and benefit provisions, would be burdensome and confusing. It would be likely to create a succession of political problems when, like VAT on household fuel, particular changes were seen as targeted at particular sections of society. A more comprehensive approach is needed, based on a small number of major taxes and benefits applied 'upstream.' These will be universal in their impact—clearly not targeting one section of society rather than another—and systematically designed to provide incentives throughout all aspects of economic life, encouraging activities that add value and discouraging activities that subtract it.

The shape of such a comprehensive reform package, to be phased in over a period of ten to twenty years, can be outlined, as follows, to include:

- phasing out taxes on incomes (including social insurance contributions), profits, and value added tax, and perhaps eventually also taxes on financial capital;
- replacing them with taxes and charges on the use of natural and social sources of wealth, including taxes on:
  - fossil-fuel and nuclear energy at source,
  - the rental site value of land (on the lines originally advocated by Tom Paine and, in much greater depth a century later, by the American economist Henry George), and
  - the use of other common resources such as the capacity of the environment to absorb pollution and waste; and
- phasing in a Citizen's Income, paid to all citizens as a right, which would replace existing tax allowances and many existing social benefits.

By transforming the bulk of today's welfare payments into payments reflecting each citizen's entitlement to a share in the value of common resources, this package of reforms would address one of the root causes of economic and social inequality underlying the more immediate causes of unemployment, poverty and social exclusion today: the fact that citizens do not now enjoy an equal share of those common resources and values. Many enjoy much less, and others much more, than their fair share.

The international application of the same principle has been urged by some Third World advocates, who argue that what is now regarded as aid should be transformed into payments reflecting the entitlement of every world citizen to a fair share of the value of the world's common resources, including the global atmosphere's capacity to absorb pollution. Each nation, for example, should pay pro rata for its emissions of carbon dioxide, and the revenue should be recycled to nations on a per capita basis, reflecting the size of their populations.

Returning to the national level, there are a number of specific arguments, in addition to those already mentioned, for a reform package on these lines. They concern: universality of treatment; easier access to housing and land for people now priced out of them; improved opportunities for useful work of all kinds; less volatile economic cycles, with the peaks and troughs smoothed out; and encouragement to greater local economic and social self-reliance. One point in particular must be emphasised. It concerns the distributive effects of the proposed changes.

Ecotax reform, if limited to replacing taxes on employment, incomes and profits with environmental taxes and charges, will be regressive, in the sense of hitting poorer people relatively harder than richer ones. For example, non-taxpayers will gain nothing from reduction or abolition of income tax; and since poorer people spend a larger proportion of their income on household energy than richer ones, a high level of tax on energy will tend to hit them harder. The same goes for other environmental charges, e.g. charges imposed on vehicles in cities in order to reduce urban traffic congestion. These regressive effects will have to be corrected. This is an important reason for combining land-rent taxation and Citizen's Income with ecotax reform. The land tax will tend to raise the housing costs of richer people and reduce the income they derive from rental values—in the form of salaries and other earnings, dividends, interest, rents, and capital appreciation—relatively more than the housing costs and incomes of poorer people. And the Citizen's Income will be worth relatively more to poorer people.

A NEW SOCIAL COMPACT

So much for the main components of the reform package needed to deal with the growing problems of the present taxation and benefits systems. What vision does the package reflect?

The vision is of a people-centred society—less employer-centred and state-centred than today. Its citizens, more equal with one another in esteem, capability and material conditions of life than now, would all be entitled to their fair share in the common resources and values created by nature and society as a whole.

It would be a society:

• that rewards people—not taxes them—for the useful work that they and their organisations do, for the value they add, and for what they contribute to the common good;

- in which the amounts that people and organisations are required to pay to the public revenue reflect the value they subtract by the use of 'common' resources; and
- in which all citizens are equally entitled to share in the annual revenue so raised, partly by way of services provided at public expense and partly by way of a Citizen's Income.

While citizens of such a society would find it easier to get paid work, they would no longer be as dependent as they are now on employers to provide them with incomes and organise work for them. The modern class division between employers and employees would fade—as the old master/slave and lord/serf relationships of ancient and medieval societies have faded. It would become normal for people to work for themselves and one another. It would become a central aim of public policy to enable people to manage their own working lives.

The social compact of the employment age is now breaking down. The time is passing when the great majority of citizens, excluded from access to the means of production on their own account and from their share of common resources and values, could nevertheless depend on employers to provide them with adequate incomes in exchange for work, and on the state for special benefit payments to see them through exceptional periods of unemployment. A new, post-modern social compact must take its place, that will encourage all citizens to take greater responsibility for themselves and the contribution they owe to society. In exchange, it will recognise their right to their share of the 'commons'. and so enable them to become less dependent than they are today on employers and officials of the state.

I am not suggesting that a radical reform of today's tax and benefit structures is the only thing needed to establish this new social compact. But it certainly has a key part to play.

January 1996

Epilogue

There is no tidy rounding off or neat ending. But let us briefly take stock.

The vision of a future that fosters self-reliance and enables people to develop themselves has been voiced by increasing numbers of like-minded men and women over the past twenty years. It now influences mainstream thinking and mainstream agendas to some extent.

There has been a decline in confidence in conventional approaches to the worldwide problems of poverty, unemployment, social breakdown and ecological destruction. Public opinion is becoming increasingly sceptical about the capacity of governments and other established institutions to deal with these problems. Non-governmental organisations (NGOs) and people's movements around the world are campaigning with increasing vigour for alternatives.[1] Political rhetoric, on the Left now as well as on the Right, favours policies that will foster self-reliance, not reinforce dependency.

But there is still no general understanding that the basic questions are: What kind of society, and what kind of world, do we want? Do we want a society that fosters self-reliance and equality, or one that reinforces dependency? In deciding what to do or whether a particular initiative is a good one, it still is not generally accepted that the touchstone is: How can the people involved in this problem acquire the capacity to deal with it for themselves? Will this initiative empower all the people affected by it to become more self-reliant?

Nor is it yet widely understood that a principal cause of dependency—and of the poverty, unemployment, social exclusion and environmental damage that it causes—has been the 'enclosure' by rich and powerful people and organisations of more than their fair share of common resources and values, and the exclusion of the majority of people from them. The enclosure of land and the consequent conversion of peasants into paid labourers (see Chapter 4) was a key feature of the early stage of modern economic development, and the same process still continues in 'developing' countries today. Reversing the effects of enclosure will, as suggested in Chapter 16, be a

---

[1] For example, *The Politics of the Real World*, Earthscan 1996 (written by Michael Jacobs), is a statement of concern by over thirty of the UK's leading voluntary and campaigning organisations.

key feature of post-modern liberation from dependency. No longer will arguments of logic or justice be found—only selfish arguments will remain—for allowing some people to continue enjoying much more than their fair share of the commons without paying for it. The demands of economic efficiency, social cohesion, environmental sustainability and quality of life, as well as fairness and justice, will all be seen to require an end to the private enclosure of common resources.[2]

Some relevant measures towards such an end—the replacement of taxes on employment by environmental taxes, the reduction of taxes on income, and the need to rationalise social benefits—are already on the agenda at the European level and in European nations. But they still have to be understood as potential steps towards recognising the following rights for all citizens:

- first (in the form of a Citizen's Income), the right to an equal share in the commons created by nature or society at large, and
- second (by ceasing to tax employment, incomes and value added), the right to enjoy to the full the values people themselves create by their own work and skill and enterprise.[3]

This combination of common and individual rights is one point on which my thinking has developed over this twenty-year span, as I have sought to work through various implications of a systemic, worldwide shift from dependency to self-reliance. There are two other topics—the reform of institutional structures and the pace of change—on which I should make some concluding comments.

INSTITUTIONAL CHANGE

As an energetic institutional reformer in the 1960s and early 1970s,[4] I had come to see that, without more citizen involvement, reform was always likely

---

[2] The psychological and sociocultural factors that lead to some people seeking dominance and others being content with dependence must not be ignored, of course. But they are hugely reinforced if, by excluding the majority of citizens and nations from their share of the commons, national and global institutions make them dependent for their livelihoods on people and organisations and nations richer and stronger than themselves.

[3] The first of these rights will modify the right to unlimited accumulation of property at the cost of depriving other people of their rightful share of the 'goods of nature'. John Locke argued for that right in the 17th century, and it has underpinned modern free-market capitalism. The first and second of the two new rights in combination will help to strengthen, in a post-Marxist world, the ability of workers to claim their right to share in the 'surplus value' which their work creates.

[4] James Robertson, *Reform of British Central Government*, Chatto & Windus and Charles Knight, 1971.

to be too little and too late, and often misconceived. Existing leaders whose powers and influence, skills and and self-esteem, are linked to today's ways of life and thought and organisation, are strongly motivated to ignore and conceal the need for radical change and to discourage serious practical study and discussion about the form it should take. Even when the need for some change is accepted, reform remains largely an insiders' game, in which the minority section of the population that operates within the superstructure—politicians, top industrialists and financiers, government officials and other professionals and careerists—continue the ongoing competition amongst themselves for promotion and influence and power over the rest of society. So reform tends to happen only when it is long overdue, and then in a hurry, in an atmosphere of intrigue, and without full public understanding of what is involved.

So I was ready to see that, instead of shuffling institutional functions around, a more important and more fundamental question was: How, as citizens, can we liberate ourselves from our present degree of dependency on the institutional superstructure as a whole? The enthusiasm with which I embraced this new insight gave some readers and listeners the impression, in the later 1970s and early 1980s, that I thought the post-industrial revolution would come about by people doing their own thing, without regard to the need for action to bring about changes in society's institutions. If the earlier chapters of this book justify this impression, it needs to be corrected.

The post-industrial, post-modern revolution will involve change across the whole spectrum of economic, social and political life. People's lifestyles and work; technologies; the built environment and transport; education; the institutional structures of business and government; money and finance, including taxes and benefits; ideas and theories about economics and politics and society; ethical and spiritual values—all of these are bound up with one another. The scope for change in any is limited by absence of change in others. For example, the scope for people to change to more self-reliant forms of work is limited so long as the social welfare system refuses benefits to unemployed people unless they seek an employer to give them a job; and the scope for people to reduce their dependence on cars is limited, so long as the pattern of the built environment (e.g. the location of shops), the absence of good public transport, and the comparatively low price of petrol and diesel, make it cheaper and more convenient for most people to own and use cars if they can.

So the important question is not whether change is needed in the established institutional framework of society. The answer to that question is obvious. Our institutions are crying out for change. A society's institutions, such as its system of taxes and benefits, encourage certain kinds of behaviours and activities and discourage others. One feature of a good society is that its institutions are designed to make the better choice the easier choice for its citizens. In other words, the institutions of a good society in the post-modern age will encourage activities and behaviours, attitudes and dispositions, that contribute to equitable, sustainable, self-reliant development, and discourage those which do not.

The important question is how these institutional changes are to be brought about. And here there is a serious problem. On the one hand, most of the practising expert insiders—in the taxes and benefits system or any other particular institution or complex of institutions and policies—will tend to resist change and mystify the whole topic. On the other hand, non-expert outsiders, even if they know that existing institutional structures and policies have perverse effects, will often lack the time and energy, and the commitment and confidence, to campaign effectively for change. The readiness of many Church people to accept the economic values of business and finance, even when these are obviously contrary to ethical and spiritual values, is a case in point. And most people who want to resist particular instances of social or environmental damage or to change particular aspects of the world for the better, find it easier to focus on specific issues—resisting a motorway, supporting organic food and farming, or joining a local LETS, for example—than on campaigning for systemic changes in the institutional circuitry of society to make it more favourable to those concerns.

Accepting both those sides of the picture, the evidence still points to the conclusion that—difficulties though there may be—the initiative for institutional and policy change, and much of the groundwork and energy needed to get radical new proposals on to mainstream agendas, must come primarily from independent citizens outside the system. There is an important role for exceptional people inside the political parties, government, business, finance and the whole range of professional and academic walks of life, who see that change is necessary and begin to prepare themselves and their institutions to respond to pressures for it. But the actual pressures must come from active, committed citizens outside. It is they who have to provide the motor force for the changes that will liberate people from crippling dependence on institutions.

THE PACE OF CHANGE

In some parts of this book readers may have detected a tendency to over-optimism about the pace of change.

It is probably inevitable that change normally comes more slowly than expected by those who want it and see why it must come. In 1960 I travelled with the Prime Minister, Harold Macmillan, on his 'Wind of Change' tour of Africa. As Macmillan spoke to the South African Parliament in Cape Town about the wind of change that was blowing through Africa, I would not have believed it would be thirty years before liberation from apartheid began to lead South Africa along its new path of democratic, multi-racial development. And in the past twenty years I admit I have hoped for faster progress than has actually been achieved in the worldwide process of post-industrial, post-modern liberation and decolonisation discussed in the various chapters of this book.

But two points are pertinent. First, putting out these ideas and proposals for replacing dependency with self-reliance is not about predicting when they may come to fruition, but about communicating the need and the possibility to act on them. A more academic approach might have predicted they would take a long time to build up momentum. But the current human predicament demands that pessimism of the intellect be overridden by optimism of the will. Second, although change may come more slowly than its supporters hope, it often comes more quickly than conventional wisdom and mainstream opinion foresee. The collapse of communism in 1989 is one case in point. Another is a more personal memory of my own. In 1956 I suggested that we should start looking forward to Kenya's eventual independence, and begin to train African Kenyans for judicial and administrative posts. My Colonial Office superiors patted me on the head—'this is just the kind of forward thinking we want from you young chaps'—but assured me that, in fact, it would be at least another twenty years before the question would arise. Less than five years later the new Colonial Secretary, Iain Macleod, announced the forthcoming independence of Kenya. The post-industrial, post-modern breakthrough may prove not to be so far off as it sometimes seems.

IN CONCLUSION

My hope is that, during the few years on either side of the Year 2000, the need to change to a new direction of progress—enabling for people and conserving for the Earth—will become much more widely accepted. The issues discussed in the lectures and papers reprinted here will attract increasing attention and understanding. Recognition will spread that a historical transition of the first magnitude is upon us, and that its impact will be comparable in scope with the change from the European Middle Ages to the modern era some five hundred years ago. But this time there will be two important differences. The impact will be worldwide from the start, and one of the possible outcomes could be catastrophe for the human species as a whole.

As this awareness grows, more and more attention will be given to the practicalities of change. Particular attention will focus on the obstacles to it, and how they can be removed or by-passed. But that is a topic for another time.

January 1997

P.S. Some promising developments have taken place this year.

A New Labour Government has been elected in Britain. One of its declared aims is to help the poor and excluded sections of society to escape the culture of dependency.

Throughout Europe, doubts have been growing whether European Monetary Union in the form of a single European currency can and should go ahead on the planned timetable. An obvious fall-back position would be to encourage the evolution of the existing ecu into a common means of exchange (alongside existing currencies) for those who wish to use it. This could help to open the way to a multi-level system of co-existing currencies, including local ones in due course.

At the request of the Forward Studies Unit of the European Commission in Brussels, I have provided it with a 122-page Briefing for Policy Makers on "The New Economics of Sustainable Development".

As an optimist, I am tempted to see developments like these as signs that change towards a more people-centred, less dependency-reinforcing direction of progress may not be too far away. As a realist, I know it would be foolish to take this for granted.

August 1997

Index

Index

Index

JAMES ROBERTSON: BIOGRAPHICAL NOTE

James Robertson studied history, philosophy and classics at Oxford. From 1953 to 1965 he worked as a British government policy-maker in Whitehall—first on decolonisation and development, accompanying Prime Minister Harold Macmillan on his 'Wind of Change' tour of Africa in 1960; then in the Cabinet Office. Then, after three years' in management consultancy and systems analysis, he set up and led an inter-bank research organisation for the British banks. Between 1965 and 1973 he took part in various enquiries on the organisation of British government, civil service and parliament, and on London's future as a world financial centre.

Since 1973 he has worked independently as a writer and thinker on alternative futures and economic and social change. He is internationally known as a speaker on the post-industrial transition to equitable and sustainable development, and what it may mean for lifestyles, work, health, business management, public policy and other aspects of economic and social life.

Robertson's books include *The Sane Alternative: A Choice of Futures* (Robertson, revised edition 1983), *Future Work: Jobs, Self-Employment and Leisure after the Industrial Age* (Gower/Temple Smith, London; Universe, New York; 1985), and *Future Wealth: A New Economics for the 21st Century* (Cassell, London; Bootstrap, New York; 1990).

With his wife, Alison Pritchard, Robertson edits the twice-yearly newsletter *Turning Point 2000*. In 1984 they helped to set up The Other Economic Summit (TOES), and subsequently the New Economics Foundation (NEF). Robertson's publications for TOES and NEF include *Health, Wealth and the New Economics* (1985), *The New Economics of Information* (1989), and *Benefits and Taxes: A Radical Strategy* (1994).

ISBN 0-275-96315-2

90000>

9 780275 963156

EAN

HARDCOVER BAR CODE